Striving for Excellence in College

Tips for Active Learning

M. Neil Browne

Stuart Keeley

Bowling Green State University

PRENTICE HALL
Upper Saddle River, NJ 07458

Library of Congress Cataloging-in-Publication Data

Browne, M. Neil,
    Striving for excellence in college : tips for active learning / M.
Neil Browne, Stuart Keeley.
      p.   cm.
    ISBN 0-13-458878-9
    1. Study skills—United States.   2. Active learning—United
States.   I. Keeley, Stuart M.   II. Title.
LB2395.B77   1996
378.1´7028´12—dc20   96-31843
                                         CIP

Acquisitions Editor: Maggie Barbieri
Director of Production and Manufacturing: Barbara Kittle
Project Manager: Maureen Richardson
Manufacturing Manager: Nick Sklitsis
Prepress and Manufacturing Buyer: Mary Ann Gloriande
Interior Design: Maureen Richardson
Cover design: Bruce Kenselaar

This book was set in 10.5/12 Berkeley Book by Innodata Publishing
Services, Inc. and was printed and bound by Quebecor Martinsburg.
The cover was printed by Phoenix Color Corp.

© 1997 by Prentice-Hall, Inc.
Simon & Schuster/A Viacom Company
Upper Saddle River, NJ 07458

Printed in the United States of America
10 9 8 7 6 5 4 3

ISBN 0-13-458878-9

Prentice-Hall International (UK) Limited, London
Prentice-Hall of Australia Pty. Limited, Sydney
Prentice-Hall Canada Inc., Toronto
Prentice-Hall Hispanoamericana, S.A., Mexico
Prentice-Hall of India Private Limited, New Delhi
Prentice-Hall of Japan, Inc., Tokyo
Simon & Schuster Asia Pte. Ltd., Singapore
Editora Prentice-Hall do Brasil, Ltda., Rio de Janeiro

CONTENTS

PART III: EXTERNAL CONDITIONS

PREFACE

Every one of us can learn more effectively than our current performance suggests. We wrote this book to help you become more like the learner you want to be—productive and engaged. Besides encouragement, what we have to offer are tips that skilled learners already know and use to their benefit. We want you to know about them too.

We have faith in your curiosity and desire for self-improvement. But you need specific guidance from experienced learners to move your natural inclinations along. Learning is a process that uses particular skills and attitudes to expand your awareness and appreciation. The skills and attitudes do not fall into place just because you go to school or get a little older; we all need the help of caring teachers to give us the clues and strategies that will allow us to reach a point where we can feel confident about our capability to learn on our own.

This book is a gift to you from two teachers who are your partners in learning. In fact, as we wrote the book, we found ourselves reminded of many tips that we needed to use more frequently as we both continue to learn. For example, we both get lazy at times just like any other learner and forget to take careful notes when we hear a wonderful speaker, read a moving passage, or discover for the first time a creative scientific experiment. There are so many tips in this book that all of us can benefit from reading and studying it. We hope it is a book that you will want to keep as a reminder of the many ways in which you can be a better learner tomorrow than you are today.

The aim of the book is not just learning, but excellence in learning. By excellence, we do not mean some lofty goal that only a few geniuses can hope to reach. Instead, we mean steady improvement toward the goal of self-directed, ongoing pursuit of the questions that you and your community see as significant. We know that you want to matter to yourself and others. You improve your chances of making a difference when you approach decisions with a set of strategies that reveals new questions and alternative answers that others may have missed. Your opinions acquire complexity and richness; other people notice your contributions.

As you read this little book, latch onto those tips that seem especially useful to you. The book is full of helpful hints, but you are the judge of which ones will be beneficial to you as you continue to learn. We wrote the book so that college students, regardless of their current abilities, would all finish the book with an expanded ability to think and learn more effectively, both during and after college.

ACKNOWLEDGMENTS

We have the good fortune of knowing a large number of highly skilled learners. Many of them have helped us with this book. But their largest role in this book is their having provided actual models of thoughtful, active learners. Part of our task in writing the book has been trying to capture the strategies that we have seen them use so effectively as they sought excellence in college and then later in their careers.

First, we owe a huge debt to Michael T. Leschinsky, Wesley H. Hiers, Melanie Myers, and Carrie Williamson for their help in the design and construction of the chapters. Second, several students and friends will notice their words somewhere in the text, so we should probably mention the generous help of Gretchen Browne, Shannon Browne, Barb Keeley, Terri Keeley, Nancy Kubasek, Andrea Giampetro-Meyer, and Andrea Shemberg. They seemed to enjoy recalling their own discovery of tips for active learning. We also wish to express our appreciation for the helpful comments of the following reviewers: Clinita Ford, CNJ ASSOCIATES; Mary H. Gresham, University at Buffalo; Bruce Linster, United States Air Force Academy; A. Cheryl Curtis, University of Hartford; Nancy Mills, Oklahoma State University.

MOUNTAINS MUST BE CLIMBED TO REACH THE OTHER SIDE

Chapter 1

Mediocrity's easy; the good things take time.

—BOB SEGER AND THE SILVER BULLET BAND

Close your eyes for a few minutes, and let your imagination guide you. Try to join your distant historical cousins who were seeking a better life. They had heard stories of lush meadows, beautiful valleys, fertile farmland, as well as mines full of gold and silver. They weren't sure where they were going nor what would be there once they arrived, but—full of hope—they started walking or riding toward a better life.

Tired and anxious, they would eventually see in the distance a frightening, awesome obstacle—the mountains. Face to face with a hurdle that seemed to mock them with its enormous bulk and treacherous terrain, they continued to trudge ahead, determined and courageous. The easy thing to do would have been to run back, but a surprisingly large number of them accepted the challenge presented by the mountains. We admire their drive and energy, even as we feel regret about their treatment of native Americans and the environment.

The title of this book contains a challenge for you. We have written it because we have faith that you want to be an *excellent* college student, not just an ordinary one. We think we can help.

When we say excellent college student, we are not presenting you with a model of college life that is beyond your grasp. Nor do we believe that college is nothing more than assignments and books, important as those both are. Rather, we have in mind a student, like you, who is preparing for a life of continual learning and who knows that the primary habits of mind required for such a life require an understanding of how to squeeze meaning from the confusing multitude of facts, ideas, and experiences. Central to this search for meaning is the ability to think critically, to distinguish sense from relative nonsense.

We began this book by talking about mountains because we are struck by the numerous similarities in the challenges presented by those huge forms and the pursuit of excellence in college. Let us show you.

Climbing Mountains	**Striving for Excellence in College**
• As we hinted in our initial glance at mountains as an obstacle, they *can* be climbed.	• Almost any college student with the right attitude and training can be an excellent learner.
• Mountains are climbed, not all at once, but one rock or one hill at a time. Sometimes the going seems slow, but to reach the other side you have to keep moving forward.	• Excellence in college is achieved gradually. Many individual attitudes and skills must be developed while attending class and studying. The goal is reached bit by bit; so great patience is essential.
• Climbing a mountain is made easier with a map and a human guide to help you conquer the adventures along the way.	• Excellence in college is much more likely if you have some help. This book is your map; your professors and support services are the human guides, there to push you and encourage you to keep moving toward your goal of being a more complete learner.

continued

- The climb is more fun and probably more successful if you are joined by others who also want to get across the mountain.

- Climbing a mountain is tough work, work made rewarding only because there is absolutely no other way to get to the dream on the other side.

- Actually getting over the mountain may not be any more important than the fact that the climbers were willing to struggle against the avalanches, slippery ledges, and fatigue that stood in their way.

- Climbing the mountain takes you to crisper air, open spaces, and clear skies. Stopping on the way over the mountain surely is better than never having started the climb.

- Excellence in college is made easier by your seeking that goal along with a network of supportive peers. While conquering educational challenges cannot be done for you, neither can it be done easily unless other students cooperate with your vision.

- Striving for excellence in college is much more demanding than just surviving college. The drive for excellence is worth it because you want your mind to be better than it was when you came to college. You have seen people who clearly have developed their mental capabilities and are using them with great skill. To imitate them, you must overcome obstacles that stand in your way on a college campus.

- Striving for excellence in college is a wonderful compliment to your character. Of course, you should try to reach your goal of excellence, but you deserve enthusiastic praise for being willing to make the necessary effort to pursue the goal at all.

- The road to excellence in college consists of many steps. Taking some of the steps is better than taking none. Excellence is a matter of degree. Your goal should be to improve your capability as a learner. By taking any of the many steps in this book, you will be closer to your goal.

ACTIVE LEARNING AND EXCELLENCE IN COLLEGE

This comparison between climbing mountains and striving for excellence in college has one powerful similarity that we want to highlight. It deserves special emphasis: *Neither can be achieved simply by watching others. You must be a full, ACTIVE participant to get the job done.*

Watching someone else dance, sing, or learn is relatively easy. We can even fool ourselves into thinking that simply being an observer is a productive approach to achievement. The temptation just to watch is powerful.

But the passive approach to college is one of the most destructive strategies you could choose. It actually reduces your possibilities; it makes you into a sponge. Sponges absorb the liquids they encounter. After they absorb, they are prepared only to release the same liquid they have absorbed.

When learners permit themselves to play the role of sponge, they prepare themselves to be a sponge and nothing more! They can repeat what they heard, period. They are carrying someone else's message. Their own creativity and mental development has either been repressed or sharply limited.

This book contains tips for YOU to do. Our belief is that you can play the major role in improving your mind; you don't have to wait for others to tell you what to think and how to organize it. By trying our tips, even a few of them, you should get a sense of the personal strength that comes from guiding your own learning.

FRAMING COLLEGE AS A BEGINNING RATHER THAN AS AN END

Attending college has multiple benefits. You already know that being in college is a step toward a career, a most important step. But striving for excellence in college is based on the recognition that your life consists of a career plus much, much more. Sometimes you will be alone, just you and your mind. Then many of your more enjoyable times will be spent with family and friends. Finally, you are a neighbor and citizen. In these latter roles the rest of us are depending on you. We need your careful reasoning to help us; we need the fruits of your excellence in college.

In each of these roles, your mind will work only as well as it has been trained. Your professors and books like this one are all pledged to help you function more effectively in any role you choose in life. You can probably survive or just get by with the mental attitudes and skills you currently possess. But we believe you want to go beyond that highly limited sense of who you can become.

As professors ourselves, we want to encourage you to develop the ability to go beyond what we have to teach you. In simple terms, we want to help you become active learners so that you can use college like a trampoline to propel you far beyond where you will be when you graduate. IF we can play that role, we will have helped you see college as a beginning, not the end, of your learning.

STRIVING FOR EXCELLENCE IN COLLEGE: ITS ORGANIZATION AND LOGIC

The plan of this book is one that should make sense to you. Each of the three parts is fundamental to your excellence as a learner. The first focuses on attitudes. This section is first because just as no mountain gets climbed unless certain attitudes are present, active learning is impossible unless specific attitudes are present. Here, an important message about learning attitudes is the role that you play in shaping these attitudes.

The second section builds on the first by focusing on knowledge about how to learn more effectively. We are struck by the emptiness of advice to students to "study harder" or "plan more effectively" unless that advice is followed by step-by-step suggestions about how to go about reaching the goal. This book gives you dozens of specific things that you can do to activate your learning.

The third section recognizes that the mixture of attitudes and skills that you bring to and develop in college are put to use in a particular environment. Your college, peers, and professors provide the context that promotes or limits your active learning. The third and final section suggests how you can maximize the positive aspects of this environment.

Within the sections, each chapter after Chapter 1 shares a common framework. The first step is a self-assessment that serves as an orientation to the subject matter of the individual chapter. Completing those self-assessments lets you know where you are in terms of the advice contained in the chapter.

Next, the need for the chapter is revealed in the form of an obstacle you must overcome. As we told you, achieving excellence in college is no easy task. It is do-able, but requires your best. Each obstacle is a potential problem standing in your way, threatening your mental progress. By naming and describing the obstacle, we are taking the initial step that will permit us to leap over it.

The third part of each chapter is the meat. Here is where we explain the tips that only the best students know and use to overcome the obstacle. Again, we want to emphasize that following some of the tips is better than ignoring all of them. We intentionally gave you many tips so you could pick and choose the ones that *you* think will work for you.

The Quick Review Box at the end of each chapter is simply a convenient list of the tips for active learning discussed in that chapter.

Mountains have been crossed; you can achieve excellence in college. Study the tips and discuss them with your teacher and peers. Like any other activity, it is more do-able with the help of others.

PART I

EMOTIONS

TAKING CHARGE OF YOUR OWN LEARNING

People often say that this or that person has not yet found himself. But the self is not something one finds; it is something one creates.

—THOMAS SZASZ

SELF-ASSESSMENT

_____ I am responsible for what I learn.

_____ I like to accept challenges when I am learning.

_____ I am tolerant of my own mistakes when I try new things.

OBSTACLES

Lack of self-confidence

Self-defeating beliefs

Fear of failure

Blaming factors beyond our control

Lack of curiosity

Let us begin this chapter by sharing an important equation with you:

Right Attitude + Good Strategies = Excellence in College

Striving for excellence as a learner requires certain attitudes on your part. Many people with great natural ability have failed "to be all they could be"; many without natural ability have achieved excellence. For example, athletes who have achieved excellence may or may not have had exceptional natural abilities; but all of them have for sure held certain attitudes. People like Larry Bird and Michael Jordan in basketball, and André Agassi and Monica Seles in tennis all possess attitudes that move them beyond the ordinary. Sure, they face obstacles, but the attitudes highlighted in this chapter help change the obstacles into opportunities.

Attitudes are interesting. Some promote our personal growth. Others hold us back. An essential positive attitude for excellence in college is a "take charge" attitude—the belief that your education is under your personal control and that you can and will take whatever steps are necessary to achieve the goals that you set for yourself. Below, we describe a number of negative attitudes that present obstacles to your taking charge of your learning. Then we provide you with tips for overcoming them.

Lack of Self-Confidence

Seeing ourselves as inadequate, incompetent, worthless, stupid, or lazy keeps us from striving for excellence. Such attitudes work together to make us feel that we don't deserve success in college or that we don't, and never will, have the ability to achieve it. These self-defeating self-images have many sources, including parental and teacher messages, unsuccessful learning experiences, and negative thinking habits that we have developed.

Self-Defeating Beliefs

Almost all of us have allowed ourselves at times to believe a huge assortment of things that keep us from achieving what we could achieve. But just imagine how tough it is to achieve excellence in college if you tell yourself any of the following:

- I should be completely competent in all possible respects.
- I must be applauded or loved by virtually every person that I might encounter.
- I would just die if I ever did anything stupid.

As you can well imagine, such beliefs make it difficult for us to take on challenges, to try something new, to push ourselves beyond our "comfort zones." For example, if you were to believe that you should be thoroughly competent in everything you do, you would avoid asking questions in class, because you might ask a question that others would see as stupid. Successful learners try to recognize these destructive beliefs and resist them with more productive beliefs—the kind that will move you toward excellence.

Fear of Failure

Another attitudinal obstacle to taking charge of our learning is a need to "play it safe," to stick with what we are already comfortable with, to avoid taking risks. If we fear making mistakes, we are not likely to try new learning strategies, to put ourselves into situations in which we might fail. For example, if we know we can succeed within the sponge model of learning, why risk something new?

This is an attitude similar to that of a tennis player who has a very successful serve and who chooses to keep practicing the serve instead of working on an area of her tennis game that is very weak, and thus never achieves excellence as a tennis player. Playing it safe is comfortable, but it does not encourage us to grow. When we act only like sponges in college, absorbing everything we hear, we are too relaxed to take charge of our own learning.

Blaming Factors Beyond Our Control

Think for a minute. Why do you think most things happen to you? Luck? Your environment? Other people? Or Your own decisions? Too many of us blame everything but ourselves for what happens to us. It is convenient to see our life as shaped by others, rather than accepting some responsibility for how it develops. For example, we might see our success in college as at the mercy of our teachers or our parents. This attitude prevents us from taking charge of our own lives.

Lack of Curiosity

Striving for excellence in college requires active curiosity—a strong desire to know what is going on around us, to understand things, to make connections. We are not likely to take charge of our learning if we do not form the habit of looking for opportunities to learn as well as of looking for new ways to learn. Successful learners are curious about the world.

TIPS ONLY THE BEST STUDENTS KNOW

➡️   **Tip 1   Think about your self-image as central to your learning and as always evolving.**

The bad news is that certain self-images prevent us from successfully striving for excellence; the good news is that your self-image is changeable and under your control. You are responsible for how you perceive yourself. None of us is either all good or all bad, totally worthwhile or totally worthless—even though sometimes we may think that way.

Instead, we are complex human beings who at this particular time in our lives have certain strengths and weaknesses, certain interests and values, and certain feelings and reactions—and all of these are changeable, at least to some extent. All of us have the capacity to define who we are and to make value judgments about which characteristics we like and don't like. Thus, your self-image isn't something permanent, something you are stuck with. Because your self-image is evolving and within your own control, you can change it.

Students pursuing excellence must have self-images that encourage active learning. Let's check your self-image at this time. How do you view yourself as a learner? Make a list of learning characteristics that apply to you. Now, compare your list to a list that we have made of characteristics that apply to "take charge" active learners.

SELF-IMAGE OF ACTIVE LEARNERS

- Curious
- Eager for challenges
- Feeling responsible for their learning
- Desiring to improve their learning potential
- Looking forward to finding new information

Although those striving for excellence will have diverse self-images, central aspects of their self-images will be very similar. These self-images act as a gyroscope, or an internal guide, to an active learning process and are crucial to becoming an active learner. Perhaps a number of these do not yet comfortably fit your self-image. We encourage you to consider their potential benefit, to recognize that your self-image is not carved in stone. How you perceive who you are and who you would like to become will greatly influence your success as you seek excellence in college.

➡️ **Tip 2   Accept personal responsibility for your learning.**

Striving for excellence means taking personal responsibility for your own education, recognizing that what and how you learn is not up to your teachers; it is up to you. This means looking inward to yourself as the most important source of your learning.

Taking personal responsibility means demanding more of yourself, overcoming the fears and anxieties associated with increased self-reliance, planning your own learning strategies, and not making excuses and placing the blame on others when you do not succeed. It means recognizing that teachers are not responsible for your learning; you are. It means recognizing that you are not at the mercy of educational annoyances like boring teachers, silly assignments, poorly designed exams, inconveniently placed libraries and books, and enjoyable distractions.

➡️ **Tip 3   Focus on the process of learning, not just the results.**

Avoid believing that it is an absolute necessity for you to succeed perfectly in order to be a worthwhile person. Instead, you should strive for *your* best as a learner, rather than *the* best. Remember: there will always be people who achieve more than you, and that's okay. You are just trying to achieve as much as *you* can.

Focus on enjoying the *process* of striving for excellence, rather than the end results—grades, parental approval, and honors. Strive for your own sake, rather than to please others. After all, others are too busy with their own self-esteem problems to be overly concerned about how well you do.

➡️ **Tip 4   Take risks to build self-confidence.**

You will not take steps to strive for excellence as long as you believe you can't succeed! Lack of confidence is a major obstacle. Fortunately, like your self-image, self-confidence is not a fixed entity. But, how do we develop self-confidence?

People who lack confidence underestimate what they are capable of doing. They are saying to themselves, "I don't think I can," as well as, "And If I can't, that would be awful." This attitude keeps them from trying activities that seem hard or risky. Yet self-confidence comes from mastering difficult activities.

We need to see ourselves as potentially competent in order to feel self-confidence, and we need to feel confident in order to try activities that allow us to feel competent. One way to break out of this vice is to force yourself to try activities in class and try strategies for completing assignments that are new to you. Then prepare much better than ordinary for those new experiences.

By following this advice, you will have increased your chances for performing in an excellent fashion. The more activities you try, the more alternative pathways to learning you are likely to master; from that experience, more and more self-confidence is created. Then the next time you encounter difficult assignments or classroom projects, the quicker you will be to give them a try.

➡️ **Tip 5 Welcome your mistakes.**

Striving for excellence takes you out of your sponge model "comfort zone." It requires you to try new things, to change who you are as a learner; it forces you into uncharted waters. It presents you with both the excitement and the fears of meeting a challenge. The trick is to overcome the fears.

The most important cause of fears associated with risk is the set of rather automatic self-defeating thoughts that we associate with the possibility of failure. Such thoughts include:

"It would be horrible if I fail."

"I might make a mistake, and that would be awful."

"I might look stupid; and if I do, that would be horrible."

"My teacher will make fun of me if I ask a bad question."

You need to fight such thoughts by welcoming your mistakes and errors, rather than being afraid of them, and by using them as helpful feedback. Accept the need to practice, practice, and practice again those things you find most difficult— the things you are most likely to make mistakes at. Accept the fact that human beings—like yourself—are limited and regularly make mistakes—and that's okay.

➡️ **Tip 6 Don't let negative *shoulds* stand in the way of your excellence.**

Extreme, self-demanding, and unforgiving beliefs like the following prevent us from taking charge of our learning:

I should be completely competent.

I should never make mistakes.

I should be able to find a quick solution to every problem.

Some *shoulds* are helpful in guiding our lives, but others have no basis in reality and are self-defeating in nature. For example, if you have the belief that you should always be competent at every thing you try, you are bound to fail, and to be at the mercy of your own harsh and unfair self-assessment. After all, if you have this belief and are not competent in some activity, then the logical conclusion is that you're a pretty worthless human being. If you don't live up to your unrealistic shoulds, it is easy to judge yourself as a bad and unworthy person; and what right would you have as a bad and unworthy person to strive for excellence?

The solution? Discover, challenge, and revise your shoulds. When you have feelings that are keeping you from taking charge of your learning, look for the shoulds! You will probably find some. Then check them out. Are they true? Are they exaggerations? Where did they come from? Is that a good source? Are they self-defeating? When you have concluded that shoulds are defeating your self-esteem, you need to combat them with beliefs that make more sense, are more accurate and are more self-enhancing. In fighting shoulds, it is helpful to remember that in most situations, replacing shoulds with "It would be preferable" or "It would be nice" will give you a more realistic view of the situation and lead to actions that are more self-enhancing, such as active problem solving. The box shows examples of how you can work to change your self-defeating shoulds.

---

1. EVENT:	Getting ready to ask questions in class
SHOULD BELIEF:	I should always be competent and not make mistakes.
EFFECT ON BEHAVIOR:	Anxiety, avoidance of asking questions
ANTI-SHOULD BELIEF:	That belief is too absolute. I'm just learning. It would be nice if I could be perfect while learning, but that's not possible, because I'm a fallible human being. The more mistakes I am willing to make, the more I can learn.

2. EVENT:	You can't find something in the library that you need for a paper.
SHOULD BELIEF:	If I need something, I should be able to get it without hassle.
EFFECT ON BEHAVIOR:	Frustration, giving up
ANTI-SHOULD BELIEF:	Who gave me this rule? Where is the evidence for it? It would be nice if there were always an easy solution to problems, but I don't rule the world. What can I do about this inconvenient situation?
EFFECT ON BEHAVIOR:	Doing something constructive to work on the paper

Notice how changing our beliefs greatly changes our feelings and our ability to act.

QUICK REVIEW BOX

1. Think about your self-image as central to your learning and as always evolving.
2. Accept personal responsibility for your learning.
3. Focus on the process of learning, not just the results.
4. Take risks to build self-confidence.
5. Welcome your mistakes.
6. Don't let negative *shoulds* stand in the way of your excellence

RESISTING THE NEED TO BE ENTERTAINED

Hey, hey give 'em what they want. If lust and hate is the candy, . . ., then we give 'm what they want. So their eyes are growing hazy 'cos they wanna turn it on, so their minds are soft and lazy.

—10,000 Maniacs

SELF-ASSESSMENT

_____ I prefer my instructors to be more challenging than entertaining.

_____ When instructors show films, I pay close attention and take lots of notes.

_____ I realize that there is no reason that I should be able to complete assignments easily and quickly.

OBSTACLES

The great attractiveness of being entertained

Low frustration tolerance

Achieving excellence as learners requires that we learn to overcome some of our natural tendencies. We are inclined to prefer pleasure to pain, comfort to discomfort, being entertained to working hard, and immediate pleasure to delayed pleasure.

Yet, think back to the times that you have had the most meaningful learning experiences. Perhaps when you learned to play the piano, or learned a foreign language, or excelled at a sport, or solved a difficult problem. Or imagine what it must have been like for Olympic athletes to achieve excellence in their chosen sports or for scientists to develop vaccines for diseases. We all realize that in each of these cases, there was much discomfort to endure, much immediate pleasure to sacrifice, and much frustration to tolerate. Achieving excellence is difficult, often frustrating, work.

Now, imagine times when you have been in a passive entertainment mode. Perhaps a trip to Disney World. Watching a movie or a television sitcom. Listening to a comedian. Hearing a dynamic lecturer who tells amusing stories. Such experiences provide much immediate fun and pleasure, but do they promote excellence in learning? Not very often!

Our minds are too passive during such experiences. They are not in an active, reflective mode. Giving in to our needs to be entertained, we risk the possibility of what Neil Postman warns us about in *Amusing Ourselves to Death*. A weekend in a major city or at a lake can be a great get-away vacation, but if we seek entertaining experiences in our education, we run the danger of becoming contented zombies rather than critical and creative thinkers.

An obstacle highly related to the need to be entertained is the obstacle of low frustration tolerance (LFT). As learners, we display LFT when we perceive an inability to withstand the discomfort of a particular learning situation, such as a homework assignment, and believe that we *must not be uncomfortable*. Statements like, "This is too hard; I can't stand it," "I shouldn't have to do this because I don't like it," and "I can't get this; I give up" all indicate LFT.

What is responsible for LFT is the belief that we should be comfortable and free from pain at all times.

When we are prone to LFT, we have difficulty sticking with learning tasks that are demanding and challenging, or choosing professors who challenge our minds and make us work hard. We prefer tasks that have immediate solutions or provide immediate pleasure and prefer professors who do the thinking part for us.

The problem with LFT is that rarely is there gain without pain, and the so-called easy way is invariably the harder way *in the long run*. If we are going to walk up a mountain stream in order to bathe in a waterfall, we're probably going to have to step on stones and rocks to get there. Long-term gains demand short-term pains.

An obstacle closely related to LFT is our habit of focusing on immediate rewards, rather than delayed rewards. The problem with this tendency is that seeking immediate gains almost always costs us in the long run. Eating lots of cake and pie gives us abundant short-term pleasure but keeps us from getting in shape for spring break. Similarly, passively listening to dynamic lectures may provide us with much short-term intellectual pleasure but divert us from developing our own thinking processes—something that takes much long-term effort.

Fortunately, those of us striving for excellence can learn to tolerate discomfort and frustration.

TIPS ONLY THE BEST STUDENTS KNOW

➡️   **Tip 1   Focus on the long-run benefits of active learning.**

When approaching learning tasks, ask yourself, "What do I want in the *long run*? What are my long-term goals as a learner? Do I want to retain what I learn for lengthy periods of time? Do I want to be an independent learner eventually? Do I want to decide actively what to believe? Do I want to be in charge of my learning?

Just as is true for LFT, the need to be entertained supports short-run learning. As learners we are in a position similar to persons looking for an easy way to keep in physical shape. We want gain without pain.

When you are engaged in a difficult learning task or attending a lecture, ask yourself, what can I do that will be most helpful to me in the long run? Do I need to be actively taking notes? Should I be asking questions? When choosing professors, ask yourself how you can choose in such a way as to maximize learning in the long run. Perhaps the challenging, frustrating, "hard" professor may cause discomfort in the short run, but provide the basis for major gains in the long run.

➡️ **Tip 2   Start small, and then take small steps.**

In striving to climb high mountains, it is very scary to stand at the foot and eye its summit. What a long way to climb! But learning to climb mountains becomes much more do-able when we think of the task in terms of a series of small steps, each of which can be accomplished—such as moving progressively in small steps to each subsequent plateau, peak, or ridge.

You can apply this same strategy to learning to handle any frustration and stress you feel while striving for excellence in college.

How can you use this small-step strategy to tolerate frustration and overcome the need to be entertained? One way is to *plan ahead*. Define your long-term goal in quite specific terms, then define shorter-term, small-gain subgoals that are steps for reaching that goal. For example, goals might include persisting at a difficult homework assignment for three straight hours, or writing down five critical thinking questions following a lecture.

Then ask, "How close to the goal am I now, and what goals would represent small improvements?" If you usually give up on a difficult task after 30 minutes, you might set an improvement subgoal of 45 minutes of concentrated effort.

Remember: Rome wasn't built in a day; all the great books can't be read on a weekend; and you can't lose 20 pounds for that spring break trip in a week. Accomplishing important personal goals takes planning, time, and remembering the need for taking small steps one at a time.

➡️ **Tip 3   Reward yourself for small improvements and overcoming LFT.**

Sometimes learning is its own reward, and we believe that the sense of accomplishment that comes with active learning serves as a powerful reinforcer for many learners. However, we sometimes need help getting started because the rewards for behaviors that compete with active learning tend to be very powerful while the many rewards for active learning may be quite delayed. Thus, it makes sense to find ways to reward ourselves. When we self-reward we take charge of our own learning and make it harder for ourselves to give into the powerful and immediate rewards from behaviors that compete with learning, such rewards as socializing, drinking, sleeping, and eating.

What you want to do as a self-rewarder is gradually demand more from yourself. Break the learning task down into small, workable steps, each getting you closer to your goal, and reward yourself for achieving the small steps. Rewards should be something that you find personally desirable, such as food, a CD, or a special activity. You will want to gradually make the steps larger in subsequent learning tasks until you get to a point where your motivational level is high enough that you don't need to self-reward.

➡️ ## Tip 4 Challenge thoughts that promote LFT.

Certain automatic ways of thinking tend to accompany LFT. One way to move toward high frustration tolerance (HFT) is to aggressively challenge such thoughts. So, let's first examine some beliefs that promote LFT. When you are feeling frustrated with some learning task, such as a difficult homework reading assignment, see whether you might be thinking some of the following:

"This is too difficult; I shouldn't have to work so hard."

"What a hassle (. . . and why should I have to be hassled?)!"

"Studying should be painless."

"I should be able to get this with little effort; it's awful that I can't."

The next step is to work on challenging these thoughts and replacing them with thoughts consistent with HFT.

- Where's the evidence (that I can't stand it, that things should be easier)?
- What is the proof (that I can't stand it, etc.)?
- Why must things be different than they are?
- How would that be so terrible?
- Can I survive even if I don't get what I want right away?
- How bad would it be if I had to put up with discomfort for awhile?
- What are the benefits of tolerating frustration for a longer period of time?

The answers to these questions serve as powerful hints for how you can fight LFT. Here are some ways to "talk to yourself" to promote HFT:

"There is no evidence that I can't stand it; I can tolerate discomfort even though I may not like it."

"There is no reason that there should be gain without pain; in fact, the evidence suggests the opposite."

"The long-term benefits really do outweigh the short-term discomforts."

"It's inconvenient that things are not the way I'd like them to be, and it would be desirable to do the best I can under the circumstances; if I can't "get it" right away, it's not awful."

"I don't like it, but I can stand it."

As you practice new ways of thinking, you can start to see frustrations as a regular and necessary part of achieving excellence, and you can tell yourself, "If I haven't had at least half a dozen frustrations in a day, then I just may be amusing myself to death."

Questions You Might Use
to Challenge Your Thoughts

Where's the evidence (that I can't stand it, that things should be easier)?

What is the proof (that I can't stand it)?

Why must things be different than they are?

How would that be so terrible?

Can I survive even if I don't get what I want right away?

How bad would it be if I have to put up with discomfort for awhile?

What are the benefits of tolerating frustration for a longer period of time?

Tip 5 Practice "standing it."

Fortunately, frustration and discomfort won't kill us. We are not fragile, like spun glass. You can increase your ability to tolerate frustration and discomfort by practicing tasks you previously defined as unbearable or too much of a hassle. Be like a bicyclist who relishes the chance to charge up a steep hill—rather than the one who goes around the hill to avoid the challenge.

For example, if you have a professor who frustrates you by his persistent questioning, then raise your hand in class more often to get practice standing the frustration. To get even more practice, actively seek out challenging professors, ones who make you think and refuse to provide you with immediate answers to questions. Or if you find particular kinds of reading assignments especially frustrating because you can't immediately understand them, then sit down with such assignments and practice "staying with it" for increasing lengths of time.

Tip 6   Surround yourself with others who have HFT.

It's a lot easier to tolerate high frustration and stress levels when others around us are also doing so. We feel a sense of community and support and much less group pressure to value entertainment over hard work.

One way to meet HFT people is to seek out challenging classes with challenging professors. Also, look for people in any of your classes who seem to be well prepared and tend not to procrastinate. Procrastination is one of the clearest signs of LFT.

Tip 7   Break difficult learning activities into do-able parts.

Sometimes, regardless of how hard you work, a task in college is too tough for your present skill level. For example, you encounter the writings of some philosopher who writes with such complexity that you can't understand her without other background information. Or instructors assign reading materials to you that assume background knowledge that you simply don't have. High frustration tolerance doesn't solve the problem. You need to make the task more do-able. How can you do that?

One solution is to use your library to find articles or books that give you a simple version of the original material. Perhaps someone has summarized the philosopher's views for the general reader. Also, the library has background information about the relevant topic. If the struggle you're having is with the main text in class, look for another text on the same topic that might be more readable. You will find that almost every instructor will be impressed by such an active attempt to address a learning obstacle.

Tip 8   Compliment instructors who challenge you and refuse to treat you like a passive sponge.

Recently, we received the following as part of a note from a former student who is now quite successful:

"I want to thank you for all of your help during my undergraduate studies. As my *most frustrating and impossible professors*, I feel that you have taught me better than all of my other professors combined. While most of my other professors were teaching specific subjects, I learned from you how to think and evaluate regardless of the material." Needless to say, such comments made us both feel good. We don't present this note to brag about our teaching but to help make two points. First, students can experience many long-term benefits from learning to handle frustration. Second, instructors are human and enjoy getting positive feedback from active learners.

Instructors who challenge and push students and who spend a lot of time designing their classes so that their students can engage in active learning exercises frequently must endure much short-term hassle in order to encourage long-term learning gains in their students. Students often complain to them about too much work, or express feelings of frustration, or moan and groan a lot. Rarely do students thank or cheer the instructor for making them work hard, or for giving them long assignments, or for teaching them how to answer their own questions.

You can help them and future students as well by letting these teachers know you appreciate their effort. Remember that you are teaching professors while they are teaching you.

There are many things you can do to reinforce such an instructor. For example, you can tell her directly how much you appreciate being challenged. Or you can drop her an appreciative note during the semester. Also, active participation in class can be a form of reinforcement.

➡️ **Tip 9   Accept mistakes as a necessary part of striving for excellence.**

Imagine you are learning how to serve in tennis. You make an attempt. It flies way past the out-of-bounds line. You make another attempt; it hits the net. But your mistakes tell you how to adjust your motion, and over time you improve. Mistakes inform you! You can't get better at anything unless you make mistakes. As an active learner, you don't want to play it safe by avoiding mistakes. Making mistakes does not mean you are a bad or worthless person. They mean that you are fallible, like other human beings, and that you need to modify something you are doing.

QUICK REVIEW BOX

1. Focus on the long-run benefits of active learning.
2. Start small, and then take small steps.
3. Reward yourself for small improvements and overcoming LFT.
4. Challenge thoughts that promote LFT.
5. Practice "standing it."
6. Surround yourself with others who have HFT.
7. Break difficult learning activities into do-able parts.
8. Compliment instructors who challenge you and refuse to treat you like a passive sponge.
9. Accept mistakes as a necessary part of striving for excellence.

RESISTING MENTAL HABITS THAT INTERFERE WITH ACTIVE LEARNING

My own brain is to me the most unaccountable of machinery—always buzzing, humming, soaring, roaring, diving, and then buried in mud.

—VIRGINIA WOLFF

Belief gets in the way of learning.

—ROBERT HEINLEIN

Self-Assessment

_____ I often use evidence other than my own experience to prove my claims.

_____ I often talk to people who others view as "different."

_____ I am not satisfied with simple explanations.

_____ I understand that if I am to learn, I must work hard to change certain of my beliefs.

Obstacle

Mental habits that prevent active learning

When you meet someone for the first time, you bring to that experience a rich history. You have seen many films, talked to many people, and experienced a broad range of things. This history is a great aid in your interactions. It enables you to see what you would otherwise have missed. *But*, that same history can distort your view of the other person, giving you a quite misleading impression.

This chapter focuses on the harmful role played by particular mental habits that can seriously distort learning opportunities. These habits are quite natural; but when you are aware of them, you can better resist their attraction as stumbling blocks to excellence.

Recency Effect

For example, one of our unhealthy mental habits is to rely much too much on our most recent experiences as a guide to future experiences. We remember them more clearly than any other information; they seem more *real*. Consequently, if you were recently in a romantic relationship with someone, and it failed, you might conclude that you do not want to go out with anyone ever again. Yet this is probably not a sensible conclusion. There may be many other individuals with whom you could benefit greatly by becoming closer.

Overreliance on Personal Experiences

Another very common mental bias is to rely completely on your own personal experiences when making decisions. Because we trust ourselves and our observations, we often lean on these experiences as *the* guide for our decisions. And while as an individual, you are capable of great insight, would you really want to rely on just one person's observations, even your own? Using a sampling size of one (yourself) as evidence, when others may claim to have observed things differently, is very risky.

Stereotyping

Stereotypes are also a very common mental bias. When we stereotype we allege that a particular group has a specific set of characteristics. For example:

1. Japanese are industrious.
2. Young people are frivolous.
3. Women make the best secretaries for organizations.
4. Welfare recipients are lazy.

These illustrations pretend to tell us something significant about the quality of certain types of people. In reality, however, they hinder active learning. Stereotypes are unfair generalizations; they often persuade us to make unfavorable decisions about someone before that person can even express any ideas.

Oversimplification

Many times, when we are trying to come to a conclusion, we try to overly simplify things. This may appeal to us because it is easier. But ignoring complexity gets us into a lot of trouble.

For example, when trying to discover the basis for the crash of an airplane, a relatively simple cause like pilot error or defective brakes gives us a name for the cause; this simple answer seems to fill the bill. We think we have discovered the source of a significant problem. *But* preventing plane crashes may require us to think much more deeply about how the system of mechanical parts and human skill can be organized so that plane crashes can be minimized.

Suppose we were to ask you whether drugs should be legalized? If you think of the question as requiring a "yes" or "no" answer, it appears to be a manageable question you can handle after some initial reflection.

But if we consider the question from a more thoughtful perspective, we can see there are many issues to consider. There are many types of drugs; legalization takes many forms; potential drug users are various ages; legalization could contribute or detract from many potential social objectives. The issue is complex. And to respond to the issue skillfully, we need to require ourselves to look beyond the simple answer.

Belief Perseverance

Another harmful mental bias is *belief perseverance*. This is the tendency to hold tightly to our current opinions. As a result of this obstacle, we often enter conversations with our minds made up. For example, if I prefer the Democratic candidate for mayor, regardless of how weak my rationale is, I may not listen to your reasons for choosing the Republican candidate. But this exaggerated loyalty to current beliefs is dangerous. It can not only influence the way we make decisions but also the way we gather information to make decisions.

Again, if you were intent on voting for the Democratic candidate, you might search only for information that supported her. But you would be ignoring many other sources that might indicate that the Republican candidate is the better person for the job.

In addition, belief perseverance is dangerous because it is so hard to recognize. You may be performing many of the tasks involved in active learning. However, if you are using the new knowledge you receive only to support your old beliefs, you are misinterpreting what it means to be an active learner. When you change your mind in light of a superior argument, you should be proud that you have resisted the temptation to remain true to long-held beliefs. Such a change shows strength, not weakness.

Identifying these negative mental habits and learning how to combat them can move you a long way toward excellence in college.

TIPS ONLY THE BEST STUDENTS KNOW

➡️ **Tip 1   Interact with people who are different from you.**

It is very easy to make generalizations about people who you don't know. For example, "Gina never laughs at my jokes. She's an honors student, and everyone knows that honors students don't have a sense of humor." Stereotypes are simple and abundant. They also hinder active learning.

Active learners look at issues from several different angles. Having a diverse group of people to talk with about our beliefs and decisions can free us from the narrowness of our own perspective.

Go to places and events that you don't normally attend. If you spend a lot of time at sporting events, try going to a poetry reading or a musical concert. Listen, maybe even try to talk, to the people at these gatherings. See what they think about the things that interest you.

➡️ **Tip 2   Make yourself read sources that go more deeply into an issue.**

You may have read about a new form of contraception in a popular magazine, but what do reporters for *Newsweek* have to say about it? By reading more complex sources, you can get a richer picture of the effects of the new discovery.

The library's research databases are a useful source for moving beyond your personal experience. Look up a subject that you feel you are fairly knowledgeable about. Then read an analysis of that subject in a source that you have never even seen.

By picking an article out of an obscure magazine, you may get a side of the issue that has not been fully explored by other media sources. This experience should demonstrate that the issue is not as simple as it may seem and can force you to ask more and more thorough questions.

**Instead of surrounding
yourself with people who are**
exactly like you,

**try meeting and speaking with
diverse groups of people.**

Your professors can also help you discover varied sources. When you are given an article to read, ask the professor, "Where can I find an article that is directly opposed to the theme of the article being assigned?"

➡ **Tip 3   Experiment with role playing and just using your imagination.**

No doubt, there are certain beliefs that you feel very strongly about. Perhaps you feel abortion is wrong or that pornography contributes to violent crimes against women.

But what if you had to argue from the other side of an issue? For example, what if you had to argue that pornography does not harm women? What kind of proof would you use?

This is a difficult task. But forcing yourself to look through the eyes of another person may aid you in discovering and understanding certain conclusions that otherwise you would not have considered.

This exercise requires tremendous honesty, sincerity, and creativity: three characteristics that are essential to active learning. Avoid saying, "There's nothing I could say in support of that argument." Make yourself look and then look again. Be sincere in your quest. And above all, remember that you, no doubt, have changed your ideas in the past, when presented with convincing reasons. You should keep the same open-mindedness to change concerning your current beliefs as well.

➡ Tip 4   Examine old data.

Like Tip #2, this one emphasizes the need to examine various sources. Yet this tip combats a different mental bias: our tendency to rely on information and memories that are easily retrieved, as a basis for our decisions and judgments.

One way for you to stop making decisions based on the *latest* news report you saw is to look at articles that were written in the past. *Of course you also want to look at current information.* But remember that what is biggest or most recent might not be the best information that you can get. By best, we mean the most thoughtful, the most researched, and the most well-reasoned evidence.

Examine older sources and articles, perhaps those written before a particular event occurred. For example, if you were researching militant groups in America, you might want to examine articles written before the Oklahoma City bombing. After the event, much of the information on the subject might lean toward the conclusion that militant groups are a growing threat; however, this conclusion might not be correct. The overwhelming nature of the Oklahoma bombing might have mistakenly influenced us to conclude that there is a new and growing problem.

You can imagine old data as a treasure chest of ideas. These ideas can give you a fresh perspective and break current patterns of thought.

➡ Tip 5   Listen intently.

Finally, it is so useful to listen closely and patiently to what others have to say. Avoid jumping into the conversation with either criticism or approval while another person is talking. Also try to refrain from making conclusions while a person is still speaking. Instead, give them the time to develop their thought. When they finish, then you can address what they said.

In a book where active learning is the primary goal, it may seem this advice is contradictory. Aren't you being passive if you're not speaking? Absolutely not.

While you are listening, you should be taking mental (or, even better) written notes. You should be questioning reasons that others give to support their claims. But do so silently. Then, when they have finished, ask them further questions and react to what they have said.

QUICK REVIEW BOX

1. Interact with people who are different from you.
2. Make yourself read sources that go more deeply into an issue.
3. Experiment with role playing and just using your imagination.
4. Examine old data.
5. Listen intently.

TAKING PRIDE IN DOUBT

Chapter 5

*It is not so much what we don't know that hurts us,
as those things we do know that aren't so.*

—MARK TWAIN

*Some people will never learn anything for this
reason: because they understand everything too
soon.*

—ALEXANDER POPE

Self-Assessment

_____ I ask lots of questions before accepting conclusions from experts.

_____ I am comfortable with uncertainty.

_____ I realize that there is usually more than one reasonable answer to a question.

Obstacles

Personal need for certainty

Classroom emphasis on getting the right answers

To be an active learner, you must have the "will to doubt." You must be comfortable with some uncertainty. You need to have a "show me" attitude. Such an attitude reminds us to always question the answers that our teachers and our textbooks give us and to seek out alternative answers. You need such an attitude for several reasons.

First, reasonable people disagree about the answers to many questions, and can provide good reasons for their points of view. They differ because of many factors, including how much they have considered the issue, the amount of information they have available, their values, and their biases. Rarely is any single answer to an issue so well proven that there can be absolutely no doubt about its truth. The world is simply too complex, and our reasoning powers and truth-seeking methods have limits.

Thus, if we don't approach conclusions with some doubt, we risk prematurely stopping our learning. We fool ourselves into believing we already know the answers; and our contentment provides no stimulus to be an active learner. After all, if we already know, for example, what causes depression, there is no need to look any further for its cause.

Second, our conclusions are more valuable when we form them ourselves, rather than having them imposed on us by others. When we forget to doubt answers given to us by others, then our beliefs are simply passive absorptions of what someone else has told us to believe. We should feel best about those conclusions that we have submitted to a process of doubt. Those conclusions have weathered the questioning process to become personally established conclusions. We own them, not somebody else.

Third, an attitude of certainty rather than doubt leads to a dogmatic learning attitude, a sense that we already have the absolute truth, rather than to an attitude of tolerance of other views. Such an attitude closes off the intellectual search in college, rather than opening it up. Certainty encourages us to impose our views on others who disagree, rather than to strive to learn from our disagreements. By pursuing a doubting attitude, we come to realize that leaving a discussion with more questions than when we began it is a useful learning experience, rather than something about which we should feel uncomfortable or dissatisfied.

Despite the desirability of a doubting attitude, we must overcome major obstacles to achieve it. First, our minds are more prone to believe than to doubt, and they are especially prone to believe things that are consistent with our own values and beliefs. Also, we are naturally uncomfortable with uncertainty because we experience a basic need to know *the* truth, to know the *right* answer, to be able to predict and control. Uncertainty threatens that need. For example, if you want to be a physician, you want to know *for sure* how to treat your patient with cancer.

Second, our teachers and our textbooks too often present information to us in a way that discourages doubt and uncertainty. Most of our tests, especially multiple-choice tests, demand the memorizing of what the experts know. If we want to pass these tests, feelings of uncertainty and of doubt make us anxious. Our classrooms tend to be oriented to "getting the right answer," rather than to "generating good questions."

A further obstacle is that people in the broader community tend to respect those areas of study, like physics and mathematics, that are most closely associated with certainty, and to mock disciplines, like meteorology, art, and literature, that are associated with uncertainty. Thus, we come to associate respect with certainty.

Tips Only the Best Students Know

➡️ **Tip 1   View doubt as an essential ingredient for excellence in college.**

Remind yourself that doubt serves to keep you looking for more learning. The contentment that comes with certainty provides no stimulus to be an active learner. Recognize that active learners want the answers of experts to arouse thought and stimulate discussion; they do not want to be told what to think. Doubt stimulates lots of questions, and questions stimulate further learning.

➡️ **Tip 2   Accept reality: Certainty is rare.**

Insisting that teachers and experts should have *the* right answer is like looking out your window in a rainstorm and demanding that the rain stop. We don't run the world!

Regardless of how much we may demand certainty, we live in a complex world in which there are many things that those of us who teach can't know for sure—regardless of how many hours we have studied them. In fact, history tells us that virtually everything that experts in our society have known for sure has turned out to be disputed later in time.

"Truths" keep changing! It is easier to embrace doubt if we stop demanding certainty. Instead we need to say to ourselves, "It would be nice if experts could give me the right answers right now; but because they can't, I'm going to question their answers before prematurely accepting them."

> **Tip 3   Treat answers as beginnings rather than as endings.**

Think of answers to your questions as good beginnings to an interesting conversation. Answers are a start. An answer tells you that there is a question of interest to someone. But answers should not be where your curiosity ends.

Thus, for example, when a psychology expert tells you that depression is caused by a biochemical imbalance, you know that expert was trying to answer a complex, interesting question: What causes depression? You also know that *experts disagree*—and often have good reasons for disagreeing. Knowing this reminds you that you should have doubts about this single answer to the question and that there may be other reasonable answers if you were to ask the right questions and search in the appropriate places.

By doubting the single answer, you become part of an interesting and challenging ongoing conversation about the causes of depression. Also, although your questioning leaves you with uncertainty, it advances your knowledge because now you know much more about depression than the initial answer told you.

Think, for example, how much more knowledge you might gain by asking good questions about a doctor's diagnosis of your symptoms, or by consulting multiple doctors about how to treat some serious sickness. Remember: Doubt serves to keep you looking for more learning.

> **Tip 4   Use the library to challenge your most certain beliefs.**

When you feel really certain about something, go to the library and look for some reading that is contrary to your belief. Seek out the best arguments you can find for differing beliefs. Once you see the reasonableness of those who disagree with you, you are once more in a learning mode because you then see more clearly that you need to keep learning.

> **Tip 5   Take pride in doubt.**

It takes hard work and intellectual courage to maintain a doubting attitude and to tolerate uncertainty. When you feel yourself asking, "Now, why should I believe that answer?" instead of just passively absorbing the answer as a certain truth, give yourself a pat on the back. You are becoming a critical thinker and an active learner.

QUICK REVIEW BOX

1. View doubt as an essential ingredient for excellence in college.
2. Accept reality; certainty is rare.
3. Treat answers as beginnings rather than as endings.
4. Use the library to challenge your most certain beliefs.
5. Take pride in doubt.

PART II

KNOWLEDGE

ASKING QUESTIONS TO HELP MAKE SENSE OF THE REASONING

To understand is to perceive patterns.

—ISAIAH BERLIN

SELF-ASSESSMENT

_____ When I read a book or listen to a lecture, I know how to find the basic reasoning.

_____ I frequently write questions in the margins of my books to help clarify my understanding.

OBSTACLE

Not knowing how to make sense of the reasoning

Active learning begins with questioning! Effective active learners know how to ask the right questions—those questions that help them take charge of their learning and actively use their knowledge. When we know what questions to ask, we do not have to be like sponges that simply try to absorb as much information as we can. Instead, we can actively make our own personal meaning out of any information we encounter.

Knowing how and when to ask particular questions gives us a sense of new power and awareness. For example, imagine reading an assignment about some recent wonder drug for lung cancer. One option you have is to try to memorize as much of it as possible so that you could reproduce what you read when you are asked to do so. This is the kind of learning that is useful for passing multiple-choice tests and making conversation at parties.

But the active learner wants to do more. If you know what questions to ask, you can critically evaluate the information, making informed judgments about what to believe and what you need to know to better understand the meaning of the article. You can also add much to the meaning of the article by asking questions that help make connections between the article and other things that you know.

Not knowing the right questions to ask keeps us from being effective active learners. This chapter and the next two provide you with tips to help overcome this obstacle. It will be especially useful for you to keep in mind three kinds of questions:

1. Questions that help you *make sense* out of the reasoning in lectures and readings,

2. Questions that help you *evaluate* the quality of the reasoning, and

3. Questions that help you *expand the meaning* of lectures and readings by making connections with other ideas and with personal experiences. This chapter focuses on the first type of question.

This list is a good introduction, but active learners recognize that learning to use good questions is a lifelong process.

Tips Only the Best Students Know

➡️   **Tip 1   Always ask, what is my purpose in reading or listening to this?**

Active learners recognize what their learning purpose is and ask questions accordingly. Approaching a learning task without a conscious purpose is a lot like approaching a shopping trip without knowing what you are looking for. It runs a high risk of being a complete waste of time.

Different learning purposes lead to different approaches to questioning. Here are just a few of the many reasons why you might be listening and reading in college:

- Preparing for a class discussion
- Preparing for a multiple-choice test that requires that you memorize facts
- Studying for an essay exam that requires integration of class material
- Gathering information for a research proposal
- Scanning material about a topic in which you are interested
- Preparing for a debate

The kinds of questions you ask when you critically evaluate a persuasive essay will be quite different from questions you ask when you read a textbook chapter on a topic you care little about, as you prepare for a multiple-choice test. Likewise, the way you question an article when you prepare to write a paper may be different from questions you ask when you prepare for an essay exam.

How you answer the question of *purpose* sets the stage for how you go about further questioning. Before you dive into a learning task, always ask, What is my purpose? And *be specific* about your purpose! Stating your purpose as "to study hard" will be a lot less helpful than stating it, for example, as "to prepare for a class discussion in which I need to be aware of the main points and the reasons supporting them."

➡️   **Tip 2   Ask questions that help you sort out the important parts of the reasoning.**

Active learners use questions to transform information and claims into something that is personally meaningful. They recognize that good reasoning has a structure, or organization, to it and that building that structure by asking questions is a first step in doing anything else with the reasoning, such as evaluating it or making connections with other things we know. Not everything that you read or hear is equally important to you. You need to sort out the most important parts and put them back together in a way that is meaningful to you. You begin this sorting process by asking questions that help you find the important parts.

These very important questions are as follows:

1. *What is the issue?*
2. *What is the conclusion?*
3. *What are the reasons supporting the conclusion?*

What are you asking when you ask these questions? A brief look at each should be helpful.

When writers or speakers want to convince you of something, they are reacting to some issue or question that is important to them. You need to know what that question is, because knowing that question keeps you focused, puts the entire reasoning into some broader context and reminds you that the communicator may have ignored many possible answers.

Remember: *Answers always imply questions,* and *questions have more than one answer.*

Conclusions are answers to questions; they are what the communicator is trying to prove, the point he is trying to make. You do not know where authors are going with their reasoning until you know their conclusion. You always need to keep the conclusion in mind as you try to understand and evaluate reasoning. Questions that help us find the conclusion include:

What's your point?
What are you trying to prove?
And therefore?
What do you want me to believe?

Good reasoning is in the form: This, because of that. The "this" is the conclusion; the "that" is the reasons that are used to make us believe the conclusion; the better the reasons, the more we should pay attention to the conclusion. Thus, to understand the basic structure of the reasoning, you need to ask: *What are the reasons?* Reasons can be in many forms, but always provide the answer to the question:

Why do you think that is so?

Active learners are always asking "*Why?*"

➡ **Tip 3 Ask questions that help you clarify key terms and phrases in the reasoning.**

You can't fully understand the reasoning structure unless you understand clearly the key terms and phrases used in the reasoning. Thus, you need to study the language of the writer or speaker very carefully, asking: Are there any terms or phrases in the reasons or the conclusion that need to be clarified?

As you read, you can write in the margin:

What does the writer mean by that?

When you listen to a lecture, you can prepare to ask the lecturer:

What exactly do you mean by _____?

As a test of your own understanding of key ideas and concepts, you can ask:

What's another example of that idea?

If you can generate another example, then you probably know what the idea means.

Once you have identified the issue, the conclusion, and the reasons, and then clarified terms, you have put together the visible structure of the reasoning.

Tip 4   Ask questions that help you determine hidden parts of the reasoning.

There's always more to reasoning than meets the eye. All reasoning takes certain ideas for granted in order for the reasoning to really make good sense. These ideas are *assumptions*. For example, when we argue that this book will be helpful to you because it will show you how to overcome obstacles to striving for excellence, our argument makes sense only if we assume that you can actually use the suggestions that you read. Thus, to most fully understand somebody's reasoning, you need to ask:

What are the assumptions?

Finding assumptions is often hard work, and you will probably need lots of practice in finding them before you get very good at doing it. One way to find them is to ask:

> **What did the writer or the lecturer take for granted that she didn't tell us?**

Look for these kinds of ideas when you look for assumptions. You will find that the more knowledge you have about a topic, the easier it will be to identify assumptions. Table 6.1 shows some assumptions we found in a brief argument by asking these questions. Notice that we first performed the necessary step of determining the conclusion and reasons before identifying assumptions.

T A B L E 6 . 1   FINDING ASSUMPTIONS

Brief Essay: *Gun control laws need to be stricter. Each year nearly 30,000 Americans die from guns; the 40,000 other gun-related injuries cost the United States $4 billion in medical and related expenses. The need for such laws is supported by the fact that numerous associations of police chiefs and sheriffs support gun control.*

What is the conclusion?	Stricter gun control laws are needed.
What are the reasons?	1. Thousands of Americans die annually from guns, and gun-related injuries cost the United States billions of dollars.
	2. Numerous police chiefs and sheriffs support gun control.
What are some assumptions?	1. For the first reason to support the conclusion, it must be assumed that gun control laws will succeed in reducing the number of guns available to violence-prone people.
	2. For the second reason to support the conclusion, it must be taken for granted that police chiefs supporting gun control laws have some kind of special expertise in the relationship between gun laws and violence.
	3. For either reason to support the conclusion, we must assume the idea that protecting the public safety is a more important value than protecting the individual's right to bear arms.

QUICK REVIEW BOX

....

1. Always ask, what is my purpose in reading or listening to this?
2. Ask questions that help you sort out the important parts of the reasoning.
3. Ask questions that help you clarify key terms and phrases in the reasoning.
4. Ask questions that help you determine hidden parts of the reasoning.

ASKING QUESTIONS TO EVALUATE THE REASONING

Chapter 7

It is not truth that is holy, but the search for one's own truth.

—NIETZSCHE

It is important that students bring a certain . . . irreverence to their studies; they are not here to worship what is known, but to question it.

—JACOB BRONOWSKI

SELF-ASSESSMENT

_____ 1. I feel good because I know how to question experts.

_____ 2. I know questions to ask that help me sort out good reasons from bad reasons.

_____ 3. I often write in the margins, "How good is the evidence?"

_____ 4. I am usually cautious about drawing conclusions unless they are well supported by evidence.

OBSTACLE

Not knowing how to evaluate

When active learners care about an issue, they are interested in not only understanding what others say to them, but also in *making judgments* about the quality or the worth of the reasoning. They want to decide whether to agree or disagree. In addition, they look for ways to improve the reasoning process. They aren't happy with memorizing what they've heard and read; they want to *evaluate* it. Evaluation is the essence of *critical thinking*!

Evaluation is extremely important because some reasoning is much better than other reasoning. That experts often disagree forces us to evaluate. Our tips in this chapter are the questions you need to ask to be good evaluators. You will also find, along with them, hints about how to ask such questions.

TIPS ONLY THE BEST STUDENTS KNOW

Tip 1   Ask: "Are there any fallacies in the reasoning?"

Check the reasoning structure to see whether it includes any mistakes in logic—what we refer to as *fallacies* in reasoning. There are numerous common reasoning fallacies, and many have been given fancy names. But you don't need to know all the common fallacies and their names to be able to detect them.

One of the best ways to find reasoning fallacies is to remember what kinds of reasons are good reasons—those reasons that are *believable, and are relevant* to the conclusion. If a reason doesn't look or sound relevant, there is probably a fallacy in the reasoning. Another good way to locate fallacies is to recognize mistaken assumptions when you ask the question, "What are the assumptions?" Most fallacies in reasoning can be seen as reasoning that makes bad assumptions. Common fallacies include:

- Attacking a person or a person's background, instead of the person's ideas

- Making it seem as though there are only two choices when there are more
- Distracting our attention from the issue by getting us concerned about something irrelevant to it
- Appealing to authorities who have no good basis for their judgments
- Supporting a conclusion by arguing that most people are in favor of it

Active learners know what good reasons are and are alert to the possibility of fallacies in reasoning. A helpful way to get acquainted with different kinds of reasoning errors so that you can more easily detect them is to read *Attacking Faulty Reasoning* by Edward Damer.

Tip 2   Ask: "Is any evidence provided?"

A belief or conclusion draws strength from its foundation. While you certainly should listen to whatever someone has to say, how much respect you give to the conclusion depends on the support given for it. As you develop the habit of looking at the quality of the support, you will notice that far too many conclusions are provided without any evidence at all. You can spot these instances and, also, identify whatever evidence *is* offered by regularly asking:

"What is the evidence?"

Tip 3   Ask: "How good is the evidence?"

Next, you should ask about the quality of the evidence. When you find evidence, you have to decide whether it is any good. You should allow some evidence to influence you much more than other evidence. For example, in deciding how to react to someone's argument, you would want to be impressed by a systematic, well-designed, large-scale research study; but you would hesitate to rely on a highly biased appeal from a single expert who has little knowledge about the issue.

Tip 4   Check for questionable intuitions, appeals to authority, or personal testimonials.

Three common kinds of highly questionable evidence are reliance on intuitions, appeals to authorities or experts, and personal testimonials. None of these can be relied on without great caution.

A major problem with intuition is that it is private; you have no good way to judge its dependability. Thus, when intuitive beliefs differ, which is often the case, you have no good basis for deciding which belief is preferable. Consequently you must be very cautious about claims backed up only by intuition. You should ask the question:

Is there any good reason I should believe this intuitive idea?

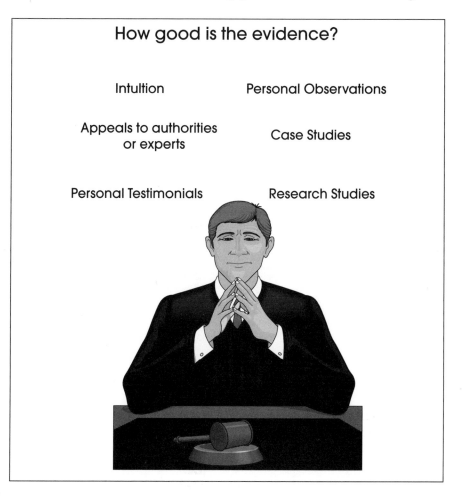

How good is the evidence?

Intuition

Personal Observations

Appeals to authorities
or experts

Case Studies

Personal Testimonials

Research Studies

Although experts and authorities often have useful experience and evidence, they are often wrong and frequently disagree. Thus, you always need to ask: *"Why should I believe this authority or expert?"* Active learners try to find out as much as they can about an authority before they rely on his or her ideas. They ask questions such as:

How much expertise or training does the authority have about this subject?

Is this authority in a position to have especially good access to pertinent facts?

Is there good reason to believe that the authority is relatively free of distorting influences, such as personal biases, values, or financial ties?

Because personal experiences are very vivid in their memories, people often rely on them to support their beliefs. However, personal testimonials by

themselves are never good evidence! They fail to give you a representative sample of experiences! Also, personal testimonials tend to be highly biased and not objective. A single striking experience or several such experiences can demonstrate that certain outcomes are *possible*, but such experiences can't demonstrate that such outcomes are *typical*. Beware of arguments that say, "My experience proves. . ." or arguments that cite lots of personal testimonials as evidence—one of the most common kinds of evidence used in TV commercials. Always ask of personal testimonials:

> How selective are these testimonials?
> What factors might bias them?
> What possible negative experiences are omitted?

⟹ **Tip 5** **Examine the quality of the research evidence.**

Research studies are usually more careful than personal observations or case studies in trying to minimize biases, and thus can sometimes provide you with more dependable evidence for a conclusion; but you still want to examine the studies closely for a variety of reasons, including the following:

1. Such studies vary in quality.
2. Research findings are often contradictory.
3. Researchers have expectations, attitudes, values and needs that bias their research.
4. Speakers and writers often distort or simplify research conclusions.
5. Research generalizations often change over time, especially claims about human behavior.
6. The need for financial gain, status, security, and other factors can affect research outcomes.

In brief, researchers are human beings, not computers. What follows are a number of questions that you can ask about research findings to help you decide whether they are good evidence:

What is the quality of the source of the report?
Has the study been done more than once?
How selective has the communicator been in choosing which studies to mention?
Is there any reason for someone to have distorted the research?
Are there any biases or distortions in the survey questionnaires, ratings, or other measures that the researcher uses?

⟹ **Tip 6** **Search for rival causes.**

Human beings are always trying to find out the causes of things. Finding causes, however, is usually a very complex task. Most evidence can be explained by more than one cause. Thus, while writers and speakers will present you with evidence for *the* cause of an event that makes the most sense to them, you always need to ask questions like:

Could anything else account for that?
What other interpretations are possible?

You should be especially alert to a very common problem in our search for causes. Too many people have the tendency to believe that just because one event preceded another event, the first caused the second.

For instance, suppose you take an aspirin for your headache; then several hours later your headache goes away. If you conclude that you know why the headache went away—the aspirin did it!—you need to back up a minute and consider rival causes. Maybe the aspirin worked its magic, and then again any number of other factors could have affected how your head felt later.

Remember: Because communicators usually have biases about causes, you need to search out rival causes on your own. This is a very important critical thinking activity!

➡️ **Tip 7   Check for deceptive statistics.**

Statistics can easily trick you. Thus, you need to be wary of all statistics you come upon. There are a number of questions you can ask of statistics to help you detect deception, such as the following:

How were the statistics obtained? How does the writer or speaker know?
What relevant information is missing that would help me better
   understand the meaning of the statistics?
What do the statistics actually prove?
What statistics make the most sense in this situation? Have they been
   used?

➡️ **Tip 8   Inquire about important missing information.**

When you encounter an argument, it almost never comes complete with all that you would like to know before deciding its quality. Limitations of time and knowledge, as well as the intent to persuade, all work together to assure that you are always in a situation where you are asked to make decisions before you are ready.

But you can defend yourself against this condition by actively wondering aloud about specific missing information that you would like to have before you make up your mind. Name the information that you would like to have, and explain how having it would give you more confidence in your eventual opinion.

For example, imagine how much better the decision of a jury could be were the jurors permitted to ask for particular forms of information that they had not been shown. All of us are in similar situations all the time; require those trying to persuade you to give you what you need for a thoughtful, reasonable evaluation.

Once you get used to asking these kinds of questions, you will be able to evaluate opinions on your own. Often instructors will not explicitly require you to evaluate material. But we suspect that once you develop the habit of evaluating, you will find the resulting sense of self-worth and independence so fulfilling that you will choose to evaluate reasoning as a regular part of your life.

QUICK REVIEW BOX

1. Ask: "Are there any fallacies in the reasoning?"
2. Ask: "Is any evidence provided?"
3. Ask: "How good is the evidence?"
4. Check for questionable intuitions, appeals to authority, or personal testimonials.
5. Examine the quality of the research evidence.
6. Search for rival causes.
7. Check for deceptive statistics.
8. Inquire about important missing information.

ASKING QUESTIONS THAT MAKE CONNECTIONS

Upon this gifted age, in its darkest hour,
Rains from the sky a meteoric shower of facts. . . .
They lie unquestioned, uncombined,
Wisdom enough to leech us of our ill
Is daily spun, but there exists no loom to weave it
into fabric.

—EDNA ST. VINCENT MILLAY

SELF-ASSESSMENT

_____ I usually try to view information in terms of wholes and patterns instead of parts and fragments.

_____ I try to create relationships among ideas.

_____ I find ways to relate most of what I learn to my own personal experiences.

OBSTACLE

Not knowing how to make connections

The Edna St. Vincent Millay poem, written in the 1920s, is highly relevant to today's learning situation. We receive piles of seemingly unrelated information, and we need to weave it into a meaningful fabric. Active learners try to weave the information they encounter into a patterned fabric as a way to gain a deeper understanding than is possible from a sponge model approach to learning.

We encounter most information in fragments; it is in parts, not wholes. It is specific to a particular issue, or to a particular chapter, or to a particular discipline, or to a particular theorist, or to a particular teacher. Our job as active learners is to approach these information fragments in the way that weavers view pieces of fabric—something that can be put together with other pieces to form a rich and meaningful tapestry. Weavers need looms. Learners need question strategies that help them make connections. Our tips in this chapter are questions that can help you make a variety of different kinds of connections.

TIPS ONLY THE BEST STUDENTS KNOW

Tip 1   **Ask: "How are these ideas connected to other ideas?"**

Ideas tend to be connected in diverse ways, and the more ideas you encounter the more meaningful connections you can make. For example, it is exciting to write in text margins, "That idea relates to idea, discussed yesterday," or "That idea suggests another cause for Y, which we discussed five chapters ago."

Ideas can be connected in a variety of ways. Knowing these ways gives you clues to making connections. The box below lists questions that help you make connections among ideas and also provides examples of the kind of connection produced by that question.

QUESTIONS THAT HELP DISCOVER CONNECTIONS
BETWEEN IDEAS

....

• IS THIS IDEA A *PART OF,* OR AN ELEMENT OF, SOMETHING ELSE?

An important part, or element, of democracy is freedom of speech; another important component is rule by majority vote.

• CAN THIS IDEA BE SEEN AS A *CAUSE OR CONSEQUENCE OF* ANOTHER IDEA?

The concept "stress" can be seen as being causally connected to concepts of mental health, such as depression.

• IS THIS IDEA AN *EXAMPLE, TYPE, OR SUBCATEGORY OF* ANOTHER IDEA?

Introversion and extroversion are types of personalities.

• IS THIS IDEA *CONSISTENT OR INCONSISTENT WITH* OTHER IDEAS?

The idea, "he who hesitates is lost" is inconsistent with the idea, "look before you leap."

• DOES THIS IDEA PROVIDE EVIDENCE FOR, OR SUPPORT FOR, ANOTHER IDEA?

The finding that many people grieve in similar stages supports a stage theory of grieving.

Tip 2   **Think about how the ideas relate to you personally.**

You care most about those ideas that relate to you personally. For example, a personality theory lecture or a lecture on supply and demand will possess more meaning for you when you can apply it to your own experiences. So, it makes sense for you to ask yourself questions like:

How might this knowledge have an impact on my own life?
Why should I personally care about this topic?

Answering these questions personalizes the information for you. It permits you to make your own meaning rather than having to rely on others to transfer their meanings to you.

Tip 3   **Ask questions that require you to seek implications and make speculations.**

It is often informative to ask, "So what?" or, "What difference does it make?" Active learners are interested in asking such questions about ideas because such questions force them to imagine the consequences of ideas. They make us think deeply and creatively and increase the relevance to us of the ideas.

For example, learning that children of dual career parents experience more frequent problems than those of single-career parents has many potentially interesting implications for how people choose to live their lives and for child-care policy.

Questions that require you to speculate about "what might have been" also make you think about the relationships among events. Asking this question provides connections that provide a much richer context for events. You can ask this question in many ways. Here are a few.

What would happen if _____ were to occur?

For example, what would happen if we make certain drugs more widely available?

What consequences would follow if _____ were true?

For example, what consequences would follow if it's true that homosexuality is a genetically determined behavior pattern?

➡️ **Tip 4   Ask questions that make you connect ideas to other perspectives.**

As we mentioned in an earlier chapter, ideas and reasoning reflect the perspectives, values, and belief systems of those who express them. Connecting ideas to new perspectives allows you to get a much richer picture of the ideas. For example, viewing the welfare system through the perspective of a welfare mother permits you to see it differently than would perceiving it through the lens of someone trying to minimize the taxes we are paying. To encourage yourself to take other perspectives, ask:

What is another way to look at . . . ?
If I were in a different position of power, how would I look at . . . ?
**If I had had very different experiences with such situations, how would I
look at . . . ?**

QUICK REVIEW BOX

1. Ask: "How are these ideas connected to other ideas?"
2. Think about how the ideas relate to you personally.
3. Ask questions that require you to seek implications or make speculations.
4. Ask questions that make you connect ideas to other perspectives.

PREPARING FOR A CLASS WHERE ACTIVE LEARNING TAKES PLACE

Some people regard discipline as a chore. For me, it is a kind of order that sets me free to fly.

—JULIE ANDREWS

SELF-ASSESSMENT

_____ I take my classes seriously, even if the course is not required for my major.

_____ I work ahead on projects.

_____ I read an assignment many times.

_____ I often talk with my friends about things I'm learning in class.

_____ I review my notes before class.

OBSTACLE

Inadequate preparation for class

College is one of the best places that you can be if you are interested in active learning. You will meet professors who will inspire you, students who can share ideas with you, and tests and questions that will challenge you. These experiences will not be as meaningful as they can be, though, if you do not prepare adequately for your classes.

Your classes can be demanding as well as very rewarding. They provide a unique opportunity to clarify confusing ideas as well as to raise additional questions. But consider the following scenarios.

1. _You didn't read the assignment:_ In this case, you are ill-prepared to answer questions posed to you by your professor. You are misusing the time of your instructor as well as the time of other students. Also, it is likely that any comments you may offer are probably not that closely related to the subject being discussed, and, therefore, you may lead the class in the wrong direction. In addition, other students will probably notice your lack of seriousness, and as a result, may get the idea that class isn't that important. The less prepared the class is as a whole, the less opportunity there will be for active learning.

2. _You read the assignment, but not very well:_ Now the danger that may result is that you make broad generalizations about the ideas you have encountered. Classroom discussions will be more sloppy, and you'll probably miss the subtleties of the arguments. Thus, you may leave college not knowing much more than when you started. You'll have only the faintest idea of what Plato or John Stewart Mill said—you may even think they thought pretty much the same thing!

Active learners are people who want to learn for life, not just to pass a test. To get the most possible from your time in school, you must invest a lot of time.

Preparing well for class is not easy. This chapter will try to provide you with a number of tips that will both encourage and tell you how to prepare for a class in which active learning will take place.

Tips Only the Best Students Know

⮕   **Tip 1**   **Read the assignment multiple times.**

Do you remember when you first came to college? No doubt you were overwhelmed by the many buildings. "How will I ever remember where everything is?" you may have thought.

Our initial encounter with something is often confusing. This theory applies to reading as well. We often become confused. We can't remember how one thing relates to another. For this reason, it will help you to read your assignments several times. As you become more familiar with the text, you will be able to put things in perspective.

And just as your confusion decreased after walking around campus a few times, so too will many of your questions be answered as you read something over and over.

⮕   **Tip 2**   **Write down the conclusion and reasons.**

Simply reading is not enough to effectively prepare for class, however. Over time, you will forget what you read. Therefore, it would be good to take some notes as well.

In high school, you may have witnessed the student who, when unable to answer a teacher's question, pointed to his or her notebook and said, "But I wrote it all down!" Most likely, this student did not touch on the most important things.

Whether you are reading fiction or nonfiction, try to summarize the author's conclusion. Then examine what reasons he or she used. Reasons and conclusions are the things you want to remember. We have returned again and again to the reasons and the conclusion in this book because those are the two central parts of any communication.

If you are reading a story, look at the various characters. Do their actions point to a general idea? If you are reading an essay, try to find the reasons why the author said what he or she said. Searching for reasons and conclusions sounds basic but it is not. *Many people fail to locate reasons and conclusions when they are told to "Read."* Therefore, you should work hard to keep this task in mind all the time.

Also try to find common themes in what you read or hear. Look for comparison and contrasts between characters and ideas. Write down any questions you may have, or things that spark you interest.

⮕   **Tip 3**   **Allow yourself enough time.**

Reading (finding reasons and conclusions, seeing common themes, and basically coming to an understanding of the piece) is often a time-consuming task. Therefore, when doing an assignment, allow yourself enough time. *Don't start reading an assignment an hour before class!* Give yourself the necessary time to read carefully and take notes. This will reduce your stress level and allow you to enjoy what you're reading instead of dreading it.

 Tip 4 Read or experience something related to the assignment.

One way you can better understand what a person has written is to read a summary or critique by someone else. Your teacher will be pleasantly surprised at your initiative. In addition, you will gain additional knowledge that you can share with the class. Eventually, others may begin to follow your example.

Tip 5 Bring up classroom topics with your friends and classmates.

One goal of your education should be the application of the ideas you learn about to your own life. One of the great ways you can do this is to talk to others about the subjects you learn about in class.

Discussing ideas you've learned does not have to be a formal thing. Try to think about how a particular philosophy might influence the way you make decisions. Ask your friends what they think. If you watch a movie, take a few minutes to reflect afterwards, and see if themes in the film relate in any way to ideas you may have encountered in class. Active learners think and talk about subjects constantly. This will help you to remember things better, as well as foster the desire to question constantly.

You will not always be in school. Good intellectual habits now will promote the desire to think and reason as you grow older.

Tip 6 Review your notes before class.

For active learning to take place, it is essential for you to be very familiar with the subject you will be discussing. Therefore, it is important for you to review your notes before class. What were the author's reasons and conclusions again? Look at your notes and try to remember all the thoughts you wrote down. This will help you in responding to questions posed by the teacher or by other students. You will also be able to raise questions of your own.

Tip 7 Schedule classes carefully.

It would be ideal if you reviewed your notes right before class, so that the ideas are very fresh in your mind. Therefore, you may want to consider how you schedule your classes. If you have difficulty getting up early in the morning (and often have difficulty just making it to class on time) you might want to consider scheduling classes a little bit later. That way, you could get up, get ready, eat something, and look over your notes.

Likewise, it may be unwise to schedule classes one right after the other. If your biology class ends at 2:20 p.m. and your philosophy class starts at 2:30 you may have a difficult time reviewing your notes in the ten minutes you have to walk to your next class.

Many times, you will not be able to control these factors. You might have to take a course at a certain time (say the only time the required philosophy class meets is at 2:30 p.m.) In this case, you have little choice. Nevertheless, you should try your best to give yourself the necessary time you will need to be an active learner.

QUICK REVIEW BOX

1. Read the assignment multiple times.

2. Write down the conclusion and reasons.

3. Allow yourself enough time.

4. Read or experience something related to the assignment.

5. Bring up classroom topics with your friends and classmates.

6. Review your notes before class.

7. Schedule classes carefully.

TAKING NOTES FOR ACTIVE LEARNING

I *have always thought that a man of tolerable abilities may work great changes, and accomplish great affairs among mankind, if he first forms a good plan, and . . . makes the execution of that plan his sole study and business.*

—BENJAMIN FRANKLIN

Self-Assessment

_____ When I am taking notes, I know what is important to write down.

_____ I frequently write questions in my notes.

_____ When I reread my notes, I understand how the topics are related to one another.

_____ In my notes, I make connections between this and other courses.

Obstacle

Uncertainty about the purpose of note-taking

The reason for taking notes, according to most students, is fairly simple. You take notes because you want to do well on tests and get good grades. Furthermore, what you include in those notes is guided by what you expect the teacher to test you on.

With that purpose in mind, *you record as much as possible as quickly as possible*. When the course is over, you then quickly dispose of your notes—they were nothing more than a study tool anyway. Many students use this passive note-taking approach—that is, they use a sponge approach, in which they try to absorb and record as much information as they can and then "squeeze it out" after the test.

While it is important to know the information on which you will be evaluated, this "learner as sponge" attitude is the fundamental obstacle to good note-taking and to being a learning-oriented student. Active learners want to know more than just what is required and want to be able to organize information in such a way that their knowledge tends to stay with them for long periods of time. To accomplish this, they sift through information as they are presented with it, deciding what is important to remember and what is not.

They may also analyze it and attempt to relate it to other experiences and ideas they have had. They use strategies for making new information and ideas useful to themselves. By this process, they personalize their notes—they make their own ideas, beliefs, and values part of their notes. Personalizing notes can help us see how the knowledge we learn fits into what we already know, helping us to make what we learn a significant part of our lives.

Tips Only the Best Students Know

If you wish to get the most out of your classroom experiences, you must choose a note-taking system that promotes active learning. Because we want to help you become active, learning-oriented students, our approach to note-taking differs in some important ways from most other approaches.

Our note-taking system is a two-stage process intended to help you become a more active note taker and to make your notes personal—notes that you will want to keep after the class is finished. First, we offer tips that will help you *as you are taking notes*. These tips focus on the following:

1. *When* should you take notes,
2. *How* should you organize your notes, and
3. *What* sorts of information are important to write down?

These questions will all be addressed in the first stage.

Second, we provide you with tips that will help you *build upon and make sense of your notes*. These tips include:

1. How to build bridges between ideas,
2. How to make transitions between topics, and
3. How to evaluate your notes.

Second-stage tips help you to learn and understand your notes rather than just memorize them.

Stage-One Tips

➡️ **Tip 1** **Take notes whenever you want to accelerate your learning.**

Students often believe that note-taking is unnecessary. The reasons for this belief are generally mythical, and are usually one of the following two varieties: Students are confident that they will remember the information later, or they think that notes should be taken only at certain times and not others. To become effective and active learners, students must learn to distrust the two following myths.

Myth A: My memory is so good that I don't need to take notes.

Even if you have a good memory, it is highly unlikely that you will remember the main points of a class discussion even a few hours later, much less after you have completed the class. Taking down notes provides you with an enduring stimulus for future reference. It is better to take too many notes than too few.

Myth B: When the teacher is not lecturing, it's relaxation time.

When teachers decide to show a video, have students work in small groups, hold a class discussion, or any other activity, many students think that it is time to sit back and relax. Instead, these alternative activities provide one more opportunity to take notes.

Because students believe this myth, they often do not take notes when it would be helpful to them. Usually such activities represent important learning opportunities that should be recorded in some form in your notes like any other classroom activity. As an active learner, the time for you to take notes is anytime you are engaged in a learning activity.

➡️ **Tip 2 Adopt a note-taking system.**

You should choose your system of note-taking based upon your *goals*—what you expect to get out of your education. If your goal is to become an active, learning-oriented student, then we believe the following system to be very effective. Our system will also help you get good grades, but it has much larger personal goals in mind.

Below, we list several suggestions for how you might organize your notes. The reasons for this particular organizational system will become clearer to you as we discuss other components of the note-taking process.

1. Keep all of your notes and handouts together, and bring them with you to class every day. That way, when you attempt to integrate ideas (Tip 4), you'll have with you all the information you need.

2. Number your note pages. Again, when you integrate ideas later, having page numbers will make it easier for you to refer back to ideas from earlier in the class.

3. Write the date at the beginning of each day's notes.

4. Write lecture notes on only one side of the page. You can then use the opposite page for listing important questions, building bridges between ideas, evaluating your notes, and jotting down any ideas you may have.

5. Use some variation of outline form. While it's not necessary to use strict outline form, some approximation of it will be helpful. By writing the main points nearest to the left margin, and indenting the more specific, detailed information, you can easily keep track of the main and supporting points of lectures.

6. Save margins for comments. Your margins are a good place to comment on your notes. In margins, for example, you can indicate the teacher's issue, conclusion, and supporting reasons. You could also use that space to list questions that you have.

7. Leave a few blank spaces between topics. You want to leave spaces so that when you enter stage two of the note-taking process, you can fill in those spaces with a logical link between the topics. Tip 5 will focus more on making such links.

8. Keep a list of your course's core concepts or terms on the inside of your notebook's front or back cover. This will be discussed further in Tips 3 and 4 (see Figure 10.1.)

FIGURE 10.1 LECTURE NOTES—HISTORY OF MODERN AMERICA

9/6/95 con't.

* • The Ford Revolution
  • Ford was 20th Century Hero
  • Both political parties wanted him to run for president
  • Model-T mass produced (1912)
    • continuously moving assembly line
    • cars were identical

Transition—The Ford Revolution was an early part of the technical revolution. One of first to use assembly lines. Assembly lines led to the negative effects of the technical revolution.

* • Technical Revolution
  • Total change in trad. industrial organize. patterns
  • Assembly line—end "slavery" of physical labor
  • effects (causal connection)
    • physical "slavery"—mental "slavery"
    • dehumanization—machines more important than humans
    • loss of self-worth—saw no finished products of their labor

Transition—Technical revolution enables the mass production of cars, which created the society on wheels.

* • When a society is "on wheels"
  • creation of more jobs
    • product. of cars, oil
    • build roads
  • pace of life accelerates
  • communication becomes easier
  • parents have less control of children
    • dating, drive-in movies
  • geographical mobility
    • children can move away from parents

Transition—As people began to be more mobile, many people left the country to live in the city—the urbanization of America.

9/8/95

* • The Urbanization of America
  • 1920
    • almost $^1/_2$ of population lives in city
    • compact living, little space
    • horses still prevalent
    • muddy roads
  • 1945
    • skyscrapers prevalent
    • cities expand size
    • traffic jams
    • conditions worsen—wealthy people move to suburbs
    • concentration of poor in inner city—urban poverty
  • heavy immigration
    • *The Jungle* by U. Sinclair

FIGURE 10.1 (CONTINUED)

- Chicago
- conditions of poverty of immigrants
- meat packing industry and factory work

Key Terms
- Continuous assembly line
- mass production
- dehumanization
- mental "slavery"
- geographical mobility
- urbanization
- immigration
- urban poverty

Major Themes
- movement of people from rural to urban lifestyles

Connection
- technical revol. and society on wheels are similar

Bridge
- Both the automobile and the assembly line were attempts to increase human freedom.

Cars
- mobility frees people from their place of birth

Assembly Line
- free people from the difficult physical labor that machines now do.

Connection
- the concept of poverty in inner cities is like what we discussed in my sociology class.

Bridge
- Both teachers discussed the concentration of poverty in the center of the city. In sociology we talked about "concentric circles" where the poorest people lived in the inner circle of the city and the wealthiest people lived in the outermost circle of the city.

Questions
1. How was work organized before the industrial/technical revolution?
2. Weren't people relieved to be free from the burden of heavy, physical labor?
3. Did people ever really *enjoy* work?
4. What does "dehumanization" mean?
5. What does she mean by "physical slavery," and "mental slavery"?
6. Weren't there always poor people?
7. Did urbanization really *cause* poverty?

➡️ **Tip 3** **Focus on meanings more than on words.**

Focusing on words alone hinders the active student who wishes to *understand and use*, not just memorize, information. Too often students try to record all of the words that the teacher says without trying to understand what the words *mean*. Instead of hurriedly writing down as many words as possible, try to understand the teacher's points and jot down the main ideas of those points, paraphrased in your own words, if possible.

For example, about every 15 minutes, jot down the two or three most important ideas that the teacher says. Try to summarize her reasons and conclusion. This will help you become more focused on the meaning of the teacher's lecture, rather than just the words she is saying.

Focusing on words alone in notes can lead to memorizing words and missing meaning and significance. Passively soaking in as many words as possible can help you do well in some courses, even though you will likely forget much that you memorized moments after you have taken the test.

Focusing on meaning, however, provides many benefits that memorization cannot. When you truly understand something and incorporate it into your life, you probably won't forget it on the test. Further, because you have made sense out of it and not memorized it, you are more likely to remember it after the course is over. Learning-oriented students reject total reliance on memorization because their goal is to make the knowledge they learn applicable to their lives.

To help figure out what the teacher means, you should be alert to certain words. Words (such as "fundamental," "purpose," "my point," and "crucial") should act as signals to you to listen more attentively and write the information down. These words indicate that the teacher is talking about the most important aspects of her topic. Learning to distinguish the unimportant from the important is helpful not only for test-taking, but also for understanding the topic.

You should also pay particular attention to the *key terms and their definitions*. These are fairly easy to identify. Look for words or phrases that teachers pronounce with emphasis or repeat. Key terms also tend to reappear frequently, surfacing regularly in readings, lectures, or class discussions.

Usually, chapters are organized around a few important ideas or concepts. These concepts, when taken together, provide a rough sketch of what the course is about. Keeping a separate list of core concepts somewhere in your notebook can help you understand the course as a whole and the individual concepts that make up that whole. The space inside the front or back covers of your notebook is a good place to keep this list.

Focusing on how you can use or apply the concepts to your life rather than merely taking note of the words the teacher says is an initial step in the process of active learning. As an active student who wishes to learn and understand the material more fully, you must dig deeper, explore more, be critically reflective, and ask more probing questions. The remaining tips on note-taking are intended to help you navigate through the process of deeper learning.

Stage-Two Tips

➡ Tip 4   Build bridges between ideas.

One of the best ways that you can move from being a passive to an active learner is to learn to *search for connections* between ideas. (Chapter 8 is especially useful for this aspect of note-taking.) Though it can be difficult, making links between ideas is probably the best way to help you remember ideas and to apply them to your life.

To make the process of connecting ideas, or integration, easier to grasp, imagine yourself trying to build a bridge between two ideas. You need to find some aspect of one idea that relates to the other—those are the starting and finishing points of your bridge.

First, to construct your bridge, you'll need building materials. When you try to integrate ideas, there are three main components from which your connections are made: key terms in the class, major themes or research studies in each section of the course, and your personal perspective.

You are already aware of the importance of the first two, but we want to emphasize the essential role played by who you are and who you want to be—your personal perspective.

You come to every class and every experience with beliefs and values. Your project as you go through school is to fit what you learn in class into your network. Integration, or bridge building, is the process by which you connect what you learn in class to yourself. Your perspective is a very important part of this process. How else, for example, could you agree or disagree with something your professor says without drawing from previous learning and experience?

To summarize, the key terms of the class, the major themes and research studies, and your personal perspective are the building materials you will use to connect ideas. No bridges, though, are built with materials alone. The following paragraphs will provide you with a blueprint that will guide you through the integration process.

Now that you have the "materials" for bridging ideas, you need to figure out *how* to put them to use. The blueprint will help you to answer that question by providing you with various ways that ideas can connect. As explained in Chapter 8, there are many ways to link ideas; however, we remind you of some of the most important ones here: similarities, differences, conflict, compatibility, and causation.

The key to mastering this learning activity is remembering your building materials (which means having ready lists of key terms, themes, conclusions, and reasons), and using a blueprint. The explanations and examples that follow should help you better grasp this process.

Similarities and Differences

Identifying similarities and differences between ideas is one of the easiest integrations you can make. Imagine, for example, that you and a few friends of yours watched a movie together and were discussing it afterwards. It was a romantic comedy. One of your friends says, "That was so unrealistic. Nothing like that every really happens to anyone." Your friend just made an integration. He connected the experiences of himself and other people he knows *with* the experiences of the movie characters. He was pointing out a *difference*. The bridge, however, is not yet built; you must determine why they are different or similar.

You say, "Well, I could kind of relate. Sometimes people really do meet in strange places. I met someone last year at the doctor's office when I had the flu." You too are making an integration. You are comparing the experiences of the main characters with your own experience, and you find them to be *similar*. Why? You say, "They are similar because the main characters met in a strange place, and I too have met someone in a strange place." *That* is your bridge! In the first step, you decide how to relate the ideas (similar or different), and then you construct your bridge by answering the question, "Why?"

You can carry out this same process of comparing and contrasting ideas with your notes. Ask yourself, "Are these ideas similar? different?" Once you have answered that and written the answer down in your notes, answer the "why" question. Also record that in your notes. By writing this process in your notes, you keep a record of the connections you make, or bridges you build.

Conflict and Compatibility

The process is much the same to determine whether ideas are compatible or in conflict. As before, you first determine the relationship by asking yourself whether they conflict, and then you ask why.

For example, in your sociology class the topic is whether behavior is shaped by "nature" (your genes or biology) or "nurture" (the influence of your parents, teachers, friends, or society). Last semester, you had a psychology class in which you discussed the same issue. Your psychology teacher says that biology is more important in determining your behavior, but your sociology teacher says "nurture" is most important.

Do these ideas conflict, or are they compatible? You could say that the teachers' views conflict (a *connection*), because one believes "nature" is most influential while the other believes "nurture" is most important (a *bridge*). You could also say, however, that they are compatible (a *connection*), because both teachers believe that both "nature" and "nurture" shape behavior; they just don't agree on which is most influential (a *bridge*).

As the example suggests, there is not any one right connection or bridge. Many links exist between any two ideas. Rather than searching for the *right* link, your job is to search for *a* link, a way of understanding how the ideas can relate.

Record these integrations on the page opposite from your lecture notes. Be sure to write down both the connection (they are similar, they conflict, etc.) and the bridge (the answer to the "why" question).

Causation

The final type of connection we will discuss is causation. Here, you are searching for a bridge that explains how one idea, event, or belief *caused* something else.

Imagine, for instance, that you are in a cultural diversity class, and the class is discussing the causes of poverty. One student says, "I think people are unemployed because they are lazy." Her building materials are: 1) unemployment; and 2) laziness. One is a condition (the state of being without a job) and the other is an idea (laziness), and she is creating a causal relationship between them: Laziness causes unemployment.

Another student disagrees with her. He states, "No, I think because people are unemployed, they become frustrated when they keep trying to get jobs but can't. Finally, after being rejected so many times, they just give up; then other people call them 'lazy.' "

He is creating a causal relationship using the same building materials: the condition of being unemployed and the idea of laziness. His causal explanation, however, is very different. He believes that unemployment, because of the frustration and defeat it brings, causes the employed to use laziness as an explanation for unemployment.

Here again, you can see that there is no *one* correct bridge to build between ideas. You need only find *a* bridge.

Once you establish a connection between the ideas, ask yourself why they are connected (different, in conflict, etc.). When you have answered the "why" question, you have successfully created an integration, a bridge between ideas. *Record this entire process in your notes.* By going through the process of integration, you become intimately familiar with your notes, you will remember them better and longer, and you will understand them.

▷ Tip 5   Create transitions.

Many texts advising students on how to take notes suggest that students leave large spaces between topics in order to prevent confusion. The active learner has a different goal. She wants to fill in the gaps between topics, explaining how they are related to each another, and why they make sense together. Understanding the transitions from one topic to another is essential if you hope to see your course as a cohesive whole.

To make transitions, ask yourself, "What are the links between this topic and the last one?" Whenever you think of links, write them down in your notes. By continually posing that question to yourself and paying attention to connections among ideas, you will find that the material from classes will make far greater sense. One useful set of possible links is the blueprint described in Tip 4.

In addition to making connections between topics by way of transitions, you should also try to create transitions between those topics and the course as a whole. By persistently responding to the following questions in your notes, you may begin to see how the topics addressed in the course are interrelated.

First, ask yourself, "Why is this topic important to the course?" Or, "How does what the teacher says relate to this chapter or section?" By asking that question, you situate what she is saying with the information contained in the current chapter.

➡️ **Tip 6** **Interrogate your notes.**

In addition to building bridges between ideas, learning-oriented students also evaluate their notes. The previous tips were intended to help you build upon your notes, generating new ideas, and relating ideas to one another. Now that you've built upon your notes, you should analyze and evaluate them.

As discussed more thoroughly in Chapter 7, evaluating starts by identifying the issue, the conclusion, and its supporting reasons. Once you've found these, you can analyze the logic of the argument to determine whether it makes sense. Chapter 7 provides you with a set of questions to aid you in this process. Posing these questions and responding to them in your notes will help you to understand better what the teacher means when she lectures and why you should concern yourself with the information.

Approaching your notes critically enables you to evaluate their arguments and to make your own judgments about them. This process of evaluation should also prompt you to compare and contrast your notes with what you believe. Persistently ask yourself, do I agree with this, and why? Record your responses to these questions on the page opposite your lecture notes.

QUICK REVIEW BOX

1. Take notes whenever you want to accelerate your learning.
2. Adopt a note-taking system.
3. Focus on meanings more than on words.
4. Build bridges between ideas.
5. Create transitions.
6. Interrogate your notes.

SEARCHING FOR CLARITY IN TEXTS, LECTURES, DISCUSSIONS, AND ASSIGNMENTS

Chapter 11

To be understood is a rare luxury.

—RALPH WALDO EMERSON

No one would talk so much . . . if he knew how often he misunderstands others.

—GOETHE

SELF-ASSESSMENT

_____ When someone tells me something is "good," I often ask, "Good in what sense?"

_____ I ask specific questions about how things should be done.

_____ I am quiet and attentive when others are speaking.

_____ I recognize that it is easy to misunderstand other people.

OBSTACLE

The belief that words have a single meaning

Words allow us to communicate our ideas to others; we may give people directions, tell them how we are feeling, or relate a humorous story. But while words often allow us to clarify things, they also bring about confusion.

For example, have you ever listened to a song and then told a friend about some meaning you took from the lyrics? If your friend is familiar with the song, he or she might have a different interpretation. The definitions that you assign to certain words in the song might have something to do with your differing conclusions.

When reacting to something like the song described above, there is not much harm in your conflicting opinions. However, in certain other contexts, confusion can cause significant problems.

Perhaps your parents have asked you to do certain chores in the past such as cleaning your room, making dinner, or taking the dog for a walk. If your father told you that you could use the family car for the night if you cleaned up the kitchen, you might be persuaded to do so. However, your idea of "cleaning" the kitchen might be very different from your father's idea of what the job entails.

For example, you might think washing the dishes and wiping up the counter top is sufficient. On the other hand, your father might have had in mind dusting, waxing the floor, and other more detailed tasks. If your father came home to find that you had not completed the job to his satisfaction, he might not let you use the car. You would be upset. However, if you had had a better idea of what your father had in mind, the problem could have been avoided.

Similar problems can arise in the classroom. As a student you might get quite angry if you misunderstand the teacher's expectations for a specific assignment. No doubt, some grades are much lower simply from failing to clarify the instructor's directions.

There are ways to understand better what both your classmates and teachers are saying. They center around the discovery of clear definitions for the words another person uses when he or she communicates. This chapter will give you some tips that will help prevent the frustration we all feel when we act on what we thought someone said, only to discover later that they meant something else.

In addition, when you clarify what you read and hear, you are showing greater respect for those who are trying to communicate with you. We want to be fair to others when we react to them; a reasonable starting point is *searching* for what they believe they have said.

Tips Only the Best Students Know

➡️ **Tip 1   Try to restate what you just heard.**

The next time you are talking to someone, try stopping in the middle of your conversation and asking, "What is your reaction to what I just said?" You may be surprised by the response. Some will probably have no idea what you were talking about. In many cases, however, it is unlikely that the people you talk to will fully understand the ideas you are attempting to communicate.

The point here is not so much that we need to listen more closely to one another (although we surely do.). Instead, we need to remember to remind ourselves of the wisdom of Emerson's observation about how terribly difficult it is for our words to be transferred to someone else without being distorted along the way.

Instead of assuming that you know exactly what your teachers intend, try asking when something particularly important has just been said, "OK, I'm going to repeat what I heard you say; please tell me if I've got it right." While you may have thought that you understood perfectly, you may have simply been attaching or forming *your own* meaning. By double-checking with people, you will find that you were frequently hearing what they believe they never said.

➡️ **Tip 2   Ask questions to clarify words that have more than one meaning.**

Have you ever taken a class because someone told you the teacher was really "good"? You might have gone into the course very excited. You also may have been disappointed when the class didn't turn out to be the way you thought it would. What happened?

One possible explanation has to do with the ambiguity of certain words. We all regularly use ambiguous words like *good*, *bad*, and *interesting* to describe things. These words, however, can have many meanings.

While you need to clarify these words when you use and hear or read them, doing so does not mean that every time you hear a word that has more than one definition you shout, "What do you mean by that?" But particularly when someone is trying to get you to do or believe something that has importance for your life, it is helpful to have a clear understanding of their reasons.

Just as asking your parents what they mean by "cleaning" the kitchen makes sense on many levels, working to clarify assignments, lectures, and explanations will help you achieve excellence in college. Whenever you are genuinely interested in getting a clearer idea about another person's ideas, ask them questions. For example, if a classmate tells you she read a good book, ask her, "Do you mean it was especially entertaining or that it presented ideas that you just cannot get out of your head or something else entirely?"

Because so few of us have formed the habit of seeking clarification of ambiguity, you need to be careful in asking these questions. You don't want to give the impression that you are trying to annoy someone who is interacting with you. With experience you can ask clarification questions in such a way that your

behavior will be seen as an honest attempt to be an active learner. Maybe your behavior will even improve the learning habits of those you question, as they experience firsthand your curiosity and your drive to "really understand."

Questions like those described above can help you get a better picture of what someone else is saying. You may find it helpful to actually use the phrase "in the sense that" to clarify your ideas as well as clear up any ambiguity in other's thoughts. Whenever you come across words like "good" or "bad" or any other word or phrase that is ambiguous, you can ask, "Do you mean bad *in the sense that* the pie was too sweet, or bad *in the sense that* you just don't really like cherry pie?"

➡️ **Tip 3   Read another source written by the same author.**

When reading materials for class, you can avoid misunderstanding ambiguous ideas by taking a look at other works by the same author.

While there are certainly multiple ways to read and interpret things, an author will often have a specific or core idea in mind. For example, B. F. Skinner, a behavioral psychologist, believed that people are almost exclusively the product of their environment. For you to say that B. F. Skinner believed that people have the ability to make choices that are not influenced by their environment would be unfair to Skinner.

If, in your text, you stumbled over a reference that Skinner made to humanity's lack of "freedom," you could clarify what he meant by this claim by reading something else by Skinner. You would then see this theme discussed over and over again in his work. You could be relatively certain that you now know what Skinner believes.

In addition, you can also read criticisms of someone's work by another author. This approach may provide you with a general summary of what the author is saying. Although reading criticisms of someone's thought is helpful in clarifying ambiguity, it is certainly a poor substitute for you, yourself, having a look at what the author had to say; it is, however, one way to get started with your search.

➡️ **Tip 4   Search for help in the surrounding words.**

Perhaps the most important message of this chapter is the need to seek clarification. Remembering that necessity should send us off to hunt for clues to meaning wherever we might spy them.

While it is often necessary to ask for clarification of ambiguity, we do owe it to those communicating with us to try to pick up any of their efforts to help us understand. A careful speaker or writer will share your awareness of the likelihood of ambiguity and will consequently help you by explaining which of several meanings she intended. So examining the surrounding words is a promising first step in clarifying ambiguity.

QUICK REVIEW BOX

1. Try to restate what you just heard.
2. Ask questions to clarify words that have more than one meaning.
3. Read another source written by the same author.
4. Search for help in the surrounding words.

PART III

EXTERNAL CONDITIONS

FINDING PEERS WHO RESPECT ACTIVE LEARNING

A *friend may well be reckoned the masterpiece of Nature.*

—RALPH WALDO EMERSON

A *friend is a single soul dwelling in two bodies.*

—ARISTOTLE

SELF-ASSESSMENT

_____ I spend time around several people who enjoy thinking about and discussing ideas.

_____ I have frequent discussions with others about books I've read or ideas I've thought about.

_____ I spend time in places where active learners go.

_____ I attend events or participate in organizations where there are other active learners.

OBSTACLE

Peer pressure to be a passive learner

Being an active learner isn't easy. Critical thinking, being active in the classroom, and asking yourself and others good questions is both difficult and time consuming. And being an active learner can often be a lonely enterprise. Sometimes, one of the most difficult parts of being an active learner is finding other people like yourself who you can talk to and grow with.

Most people choose friends who are like themselves. If you are interested in athletics, drinking, or music, you probably have friends who share those interests. Because you share common interests and behaviors, you act as one anothers' support systems. You reinforce each others' behaviors. Whatever your interests—athletics, music, socializing, or being an active learner—you are likely to want a support system.

Unfortunately, while there are many musicians, athletes, fraternity and sorority members, there are probably not as many active learners. Finding people who share learning-oriented interests and behaviors—reading books, thinking about and discussing ideas—can be a challenge. And though it's not absolutely necessary to spend time around active learners like yourself, discussing the thoughts and ideas you have is often as enjoyable as coming up with them. And sharing thoughts with others is one of the best ways to clarify and expand your ideas.

So how do you go about finding people who share your appreciation for excellence in college? This chapter will attempt to answer that question.

TIPS ONLY THE BEST STUDENTS KNOW

➡️ **Tip 1   Start with realistic expectations.**

First, and above all, you must realize that you live in a society that has many exciting distractions that stand in the way of active learning. Consequently, when you begin searching for other active learners, you'll notice right away that some people, for whatever reasons, are simply not interested in being an excellent learner.

➡️ **Tip 2   Choose your classes carefully.**

Classes are one place where you could potentially meet learning-oriented peers. So choose classes carefully; active learners will often flock to professors who mentally challenge their students. While other students are trying to avoid these professors, you may want to seek them out because of the excellent learners you may meet in such classes.

Whenever you are in class, listen carefully to your peers and study their behaviors. Those who ask thoughtful questions, raise their hands frequently, or listen closely to the professor (all things that you should be doing regularly) are probably themselves trying to be active learners.

➡️ **Tip 3   Go to places that attract active learners.**

People who enjoy reading and thinking about ideas often spend time in similar places: libraries, bookstores, and coffee shops (or places where a lot of discussion occurs). By spending more time in these places, you can meet and talk with some of these people.

An excellent way to meet learning-oriented people is to get a job in one of these places. If, for example, you worked in the library on weekend evenings, the people in the library at those times are probably especially excited about active learning.

➡️ **Tip 4   Attend academic and cultural events.**

Universities and organizations typically sponsor many activities intended to broaden cultural awareness and enrich student experiences.

Invited lecturers are a good example. Several departments and university organizations sponsor lecturers to speak on a range of topics. Lectures can benefit you in two ways: because you may meet people there and because you can learn something new.

Organizations often sponsor a variety of diversity-awareness programs. Because these are frequently well attended, and because they generally offer alternative perspectives for understanding (American) culture, they are excellent places to meet other people with more active and open minds.

➡️ **Tip 5   Work to build active learning habits in your current friends.**

You need not wait around to discover active learners; you may be able to create new ones from among your current friends. We all know that many students are not active learners. Perhaps they have not been taught or have simply not experienced the value of learning, or maybe they have decided that learning is not one of their higher priorities.

You can provide encouragement and suggestions that can move them more in your direction. Active learning behaviors make you stand out from some of your peers. You have different values and you behave differently. When these differences are noted by your friends, seize the opportunity to explain what you see and understand only because of those differences.

As you participate in classes and events, you have the potential to help your peers. Though you should not expect immediate success, sometimes a love for learning can be contagious. Some people truly would like to be active learners, but don't know how to go about it; they may not have anyone who can serve as an example of active learning. By sharing your enthusiasm for learning, you may be able to help other people learn to appreciate what you have learned to appreciate.

QUICK REVIEW BOX

1. Start with realistic expectations.

2. Choose your classes carefully.

3. Go to places that attract active learners.

4. Attend academic and cultural events.

5. Work to build active learning habits in your current friends.

ADJUSTING TO PROFESSORS WHO SEEM NOT TO ENCOURAGE ACTIVE LEARNING

Chapter 13

The world of knowledge takes a crazy turn
When teachers themselves are taught to learn.

—BERTOLT BRECHT

It is the supreme art of the teacher to awaken joy in
creative expression and knowledge.

—ALBERT EINSTEIN

SELF-ASSESSMENT

_____ I recognize that my first impressions are not always correct.

_____ I have tried to get inside the head of my professor to observe the behavior of most students from his perspective.

_____ I have tried to talk to the professor *more than once.*

_____ I *really* want to talk to the professor. I am as diligent about seeing the professor as I would be about gaining life-saving medicine for a serious illness.

When you find yourself in a classroom that you believe is not helpful to active learning, it is especially important to check and recheck your perception. You want to make sure that you've taken certain steps before you make a final decision about your professor's commitment to active learning.

Being a professor is an occupation. As is the case with other occupations such as dentists, lawyers, secretaries, and construction workers, some professors are better than others. Professors in general very much want you to be an active learner; the dream of a society of active learners may be the major reason they chose to work with you.

Yet there are times when certain professors may seem not to care. If you find yourself in this unfortunate situation, one thing you can do is drop the course. Such action would allow you to seek out those professors more beneficial to your learning experience. But the drop option is not always workable. You might need to take a particular course in order to graduate. Alternatively, there may not be another course available that fits both into your class schedule and your program of study.

In these instances, you will have to interact with a professor who appears to be more an obstacle than a helping hand to your active learning. This chapter will help you to keep your learning active in such a situation.

OBSTACLE

Teachers who appear to discourage active learning

There are at least three different kinds of professors whom you might see as an obstacle to active learning. First, there is the professor whose personality is such that it is difficult "to read" him or her. For example, your professor might be a shy person who has difficulty interacting with others. As a consequence, even though he believes himself to be engaging his students in active learning, this effort may not be visible to the students themselves. Let's call this professor "the Tentative Professor."

The second type of professor who might be an obstacle in your push for educational excellence is what we'll call "the Disillusioned Professor." She is enthusiastic about active learning but believes that it's nearly impossible. In the past, she has attempted to promote active learning but has met strong student opposition on each occasion. As a consequence, she has abandoned active learning, believing students to be either unwilling or incapable of what this book is encouraging.

The third kind of professor who might be an obstacle to you is the type who emphasizes your reproduction of lectures and text as his learning goals. Unlike the Tentative Professor and the Disillusioned Professor, this type of professor has chosen to create a classroom environment in which the teacher is an active dispenser of knowledge, while the students' role is to accumulate that knowledge. We'll call this type of professor "the Knowledge-Dispenser Professor."

TIPS ONLY THE BEST STUDENTS KNOW

What you want to do to improve your experience in nonactive learning environments depends upon the type of professor with whom you are dealing. Consequently, the tips that follow include a note designating whether they refer primarily to the Tentative, Disillusioned, or Knowledge-Dispenser Professor.

➡️ **Tip 1** **Put yourself in your professor's shoes.**

There are a number of reasons why professors of any type might be less than enchanted with students. Professors can't help but notice that many students seem to lack interest in the learning experience. There are more than a few students who come to class unprepared, turn papers and homework assignments in late, and have a general disregard for the joy and rewards of active learning. In addition, students complain about workloads and express concern for only those facts and ideas that are going to be on the upcoming test. Taken together, these behaviors can suggest to the professor that students merely want to get through a course with the least possible work.

If you are aware that many professors have these perceptions of students, then you will be better equipped to deal with both the Tentative and Disillusioned Professor. First of all, this recognition provides you with a greater understanding of the professor's intentions, which in turn can help you respond with feelings more positive than anger and disappointment.

Additionally, with such a recognition, you can make a conscious effort not to act like the other students. Taking this step is extremely important. You can help create the professors you need. If the Disillusioned Professor is ever going to restore her faith in students, then she needs to see that there are exceptions to her generalizations about them. Likewise, a Tentative Professor is likely to gain confidence to better pursue active learning after he sees that not all students are opposed to educational excellence.

➡️ **Tip 2   Shape your learning environment.**

Attempting to shape the classroom environment can be of great benefit to both interactions with your professor and the overall functioning of the classroom. "But," you say, "I am *only* a student! And besides, as a student, I'm but *one among many*. How am I supposed to have any impact on how my class operates?!"

So what can *you* do? One thing you can do is set an example for other students while expressing your interest in active learning to the teacher by asking questions in class. To do this, you'll need to do your course reading carefully. After all, good questions can't be formulated out of thin air.

Also, it's probably a good idea to make sure the questions require complex answers. A main reason you're asking the question is to help create a classroom environment in which both teacher and students are active participants. If your question can be answered in one or two words, that allows the teacher to return to lecturing and the other students to continue being passive. To make sure your questions are thought-provoking, model them after those discussed earlier (Chapters 6–8).

Asking good questions in class can help demonstrate to the Disillusioned Professor that there is at least one student in her class who takes a great interest in learning. In addition, questioning can help the Tentative Professor more easily reach out to his students, because he will have the confidence that some students want an active learning environment. Finally, taking this action might draw other learning-oriented students out of hiding, which can only help in creating a more active learning environment.

A second step you can take goes beyond what we discussed in Tip 1. You'll recall that we encouraged you to avoid harmful student behavior. You can do even more to shape your classroom environment. When a professor asks tough questions or assigns challenging work only to be met by a chorus of complaints, try defending the professor.

There are tactful ways to defend your professor's attempts to make the classroom more challenging and interactive without setting your peers against you. For example, you can attempt to subdue the collective groan by asking questions about the assignment in a manner that demonstrates your enthusiasm. Taking actions such as these can really help the Tentative Professor. In addition, as with asking difficult questions, you might draw out students who also are anything but disappointed with a challenging question or assignment.

➡️ **Tip 3   Reach out to the professor.**

Reaching out to the Tentative Professor may encourage him to be more interactive, an element essential to an active learning environment. Similarly, reaching out to the Disillusioned Professor in a way that expresses interest in ideas may help restore her faith in students. Reaching out to the Knowledge-Dispenser Professor may enable you to take advantage of someone who may be a rich source of ideas for you.

One of the easiest ways to extend a learning-oriented hand to your professor is to approach the professor after class and ask him for extra reading related to the course material. For example, you might ask your professor where you can find a criticism of a particular idea or theory that you have encountered in your course reading. Alternatively, you might ask for a source that provides a more thorough treatment of a concept from the course.

Another step you can take to reach out to your professor is to pay a visit to her office. However, this should not be a visit in which you stop by just to chat. Instead, prepare a thoughtful and important question having to do with the course material. Then you and the professor can discuss the question in depth. This out-reaching on your part can be especially effective with a shy professor, because the social demands of the meeting are not great.

Yet another way to reach out to your professor probably requires the most effort but also might yield the greatest payoff. Your professor is both a teacher and a scholar. Recognize this fact and seek out the part of his academic interests that does not come out in class, namely his writing and reading. If you find something that interests you, make it a point to engage your professor in a discussion about that particular article or book.

⇨ Tip 4 Seek out other active learners in the class.

If you're disenchanted with your professor's neglect of active learning, then you are probably not alone. Consequently, a good source for creating and sustaining active learning in such a class is other students.

To identify those students interested in active learning, begin by reflecting on your own frustrations. Think about how these affect your behavior in class. Now, look around the room during class. Those of your peers who exhibit similar behaviors may be doing so because of the very same frustrations.

For example, if somebody, like yourself, has tried on occasion to ask the professor thoughtful questions only to be disappointed, then he might be interested in a more substantial engagement with the ideas of the course. Seek him out and find out if this is the case. If it is, then attempt to start discussions with him that will allow both of you to take a more active approach to learning the course material.

By talking outside of class, even if only briefly, you will get the opportunity to have some active engagement with the course material. You and your fellow active learner can compare reactions to the readings and lectures and analyze both in terms of their quality. This dialogue will permit you to have some active involvement with the class material.

⇨ Tip 5 Stay active during lectures.

In situations where the professor predominately lectures, it is important that you stay active during these lectures. One form of productive activity is the note-taking strategy of Chapter 10. If you do not do so, then your learning experience in that particular classroom will be little more than the passive acceptance of information.

Staying active during lectures is a matter of not treating your professor's words simply as truths to be memorized. You can do this by taking the proper frame of mind with you to class. It would be easy to transfer almost unthinkingly the words of your professor to the paper in front of you. However, if you want to keep your learning active, then you must resist this temptation.

A good method of resistance is to go to each and every class with the intention of critically assessing what your professor says. It might be helpful to keep in mind the questions discussed in Chapter 7 of this book. In fact, you may want to bring a list of them with you to class. Asking yourself these questions will keep your learning more active by constantly challenging you both to follow and to assess your professor's reasoning.

To aid you in doing this questioning, you may want to keep an extra notebook. In this notebook, you can record a list of questions and concerns about what was said in class. Then, you can address these questions and concerns by talking either to the professor or to other classmates or by further reading.

QUICK REVIEW BOX

1. Put yourself in your professor's shoes.
2. Shape your learning environment.
3. Reach out to the professor.
4. Seek out other active learners in the class.
5. Stay active during lectures.

DISCOVERING MULTIPLE PERSPECTIVES

14

Chapter

Chief among our gains must reckoned this
possibility of choice, the recognition of many possible
ways of life, where other civilizations have recognized
only one. Where other civilizations give a satisfactory
outlet to only one temperamental type, . . . , a
civilization in which there are many standards offers
a possibility of satisfactory adjustment to individuals
of many temperamental types, of diverse gifts, and
varying interests.

—MARGARET MEAD

People only see what they are prepared to see.

—RALPH WALDO EMERSON

SELF-ASSESSMENT

_____ I notice that people disagree about most issues.

_____ I recognize that all of us, including professors and those who write textbooks, think, speak, and act from a particular perspective.

_____ When I encounter conflicting points of view, I do not decide right away that one is "correct," while the rest are "wrong."

_____ I am suspicious of those who want to give me "the truth."

_____ When somebody says they are giving me "the facts," I wonder not only about the quality of those facts but also whether important ones have been neglected.

OBSTACLE

Knowing only one or two perspectives

There are many ways to look at almost everything that is significant in our lives. Just look at the diversity in viewpoints among your professors! One famous psychologist testifies in court that a person is dangerous to the community, while another psychologist says that he wouldn't mind if the same person babysat his kids.

Why this disagreement? Perhaps the most important reason is the existence of multiple perspectives. Human beings do not share one single vision about what a good life is, how we should live, or what is important to study while we live. Instead, they disagree among themselves about these most significant of questions. Our way of looking at life and its purpose forms our perspective, something that guides us as we see, hear, and speak.

As a learning sponge, you have little control over what you learn—that is, what you accept or reject as being true. Rather than deciding to accept or reject, sponges nod "yes" to everything. Constant concern for multiple perspectives reminds us to wait before deciding. Have we found and listened to multiple perspectives about this issue?

Our task in this chapter is one that activates your learning by broadening your vision. As you become more aware of multiple perspectives, you will be amazed at the rich possibilities from which you can increasingly choose. Your study of multiple perspectives enlarges the range of decisions you can make; once you know about optional viewpoints, *you can evaluate them* and decide for yourself what to believe rather than just accepting as truth whatever people tell you, or just as bad, rejecting all viewpoints as unimportant.

Once you begin to see that every viewpoint is one viewpoint among many possible ones, then you'll no longer feel the frustration of seeking one perfect conclusion—the Truth. It's probably best that you give up that search anyway, because as Einstein once said, "Those who make claims to holding Truth and knowledge are shipwrecked by the laughter of the gods." It's better that you keep your ship afloat.

Without constant work on our part, we tend to accept what we hear or read without questioning it. This blind acceptance of the truth is dangerous for two reasons. First, it makes you a passive rather than an active learner. Second, sponge-like acceptance of viewpoints increases the likelihood that you will be both con-fused and frustrated when you encounter conflicting points of view. By focusing on the search for multiple perspectives, you will naturally run into differing con-clusions. They will be unavoidable.

If you want to develop your awareness of and attention to different per-spectives, then you need to know three things about multiple perspectives: 1) what causes them to exist, 2) what they look like, and 3) where you can find them. The following tips deal with each of these in turn.

TIPS ONLY THE BEST STUDENTS KNOW

➡️ **Tip 1**   **Understand that an expert has *a* perspective.**

There are several reasons why a professor or author has a certain perspec-tive. First, not everybody in a discipline is trained exactly the same way. Take psychology, for example. Some psychology professors have been trained in the tradition of Sigmund Freud, others in the tradition of B. F. Skinner, and still oth-ers in the tradition of Jean Piaget.

You don't need to know what characterizes these different schools of psy-chology in order to grasp what's significant about this process. Freud, Skinner, and Piaget each took a different approach to psychology. As a consequence, a psychologist trained in the Freudian tradition will probably have a different per-spective from one trained in Skinner's way of thinking.

Professors also get their individual points of view from their ideas about how the world should be. These ideas are derived from different visions of what the world should be like.

For example, suppose that there are two physics professors. Both are sched-uled to talk about nuclear power to a group of science students. The first one, Fred, feels very strongly that we should stop using nuclear energy immediately. The other professor, Marie, is a strong supporter of nuclear power. Don't you think that Fred and Marie's lectures on nuclear power might be very different? Fred and Marie will look at the question of the use of nuclear power from *different* perspectives.

➡️ **Tip 2**   **Be aware that facts don't speak for themselves.**

It's hard enough to recognize that experts disagree. It's even tougher for you to discover multiple points of view when either your professor or your text suggests a fact or a set of facts. After all, aren't "the facts" real and certain in a way that a perspective is not?

The answer to this question is "not exactly." Facts do *not* speak for themselves. Somebody has to select, state, organize, and interpret the fact or facts. In doing so, the person's own perspective counts.

Suppose that workers at an automobile plant go on a massive strike. They do so because the managers at the plant drastically cut their wages and took away their health care benefits. During the strike, a few of the workers get rather violent and injure three people still working in the plant. The police are called in, and the strike is ended. The workers do not win back either their original wages or their health care benefits.

The above are "the facts" of what happened. Even if two people stick to these facts, they can give entirely different accounts of what happened. They do so by selecting certain facts to tell.

HANK:	"Let me give you the facts. The auto plant cut its workers wages and health care benefits. The union went on a strike and a few of the workers got violent. Rather than arrest those few workers, the police shut the whole strike down. Can you believe it?! It's another example of a union getting silenced before it gets its understandable complaints heard."
PRISCILLA:	"Let me give you the facts. Some workers at the auto plant down the street felt that they were getting cheated when the company cut their wages, so they went on strike. Like so many other strikes, this one got violent. The police had to come in and break it up. And it's a good thing they did, too! Otherwise, the clear message would be that it's okay to use organized violence to get your voice heard."

By selecting the facts that they did, Hank and Priscilla give very different points of view about the strike. By keeping this example in mind, you can see how the facts that your professor and texts talk about represent a certain point of view.

Two people do not need to select different facts in order to express different viewpoints. Instead, they can state the same fact in a different manner. As the example below illustrates, the same fact can take on a whole different meaning depending on how it is stated.

RAMONE:	In spite of the demands of international competition, we as a nation still managed to lift 30% of low-income people above the poverty line.
BRIDGET:	Despite our wealth of resources, we lifted a mere 30% of our nation's low-income population above the poverty line.

Notice that although Ramone and Bridget use *the exact same fact* (30% lifted above poverty line), what this fact says is quite different according to the speaker's perspective. Ramone suggests that the amount of people that were helped out of poverty was a great accomplishment. At the same time, Bridget says the accomplishment is not that great at all.

At this point, you might be thinking that the number of different points of view is limited to two. If you do, then we have to accept part of the responsibility for that. After all, we've been the ones giving you completely opposite points of view to illustrate multiple perspectives.

However, there is a reason why this chapter focuses on *multiple* perspectives rather than *two* perspectives. The possible number of believable perspectives that can be held on a topic is by no means limited to two.

Tip 3   Remember that perspectives are alike or different by degree.

Sure, perspectives are different. But how different are they?

Look around you. Across the world there are a large number of political parties. There is the Green party in Germany, the Social Democrats in Canada, and the Republicans in the United States. All represent different approaches to how a country should be governed.

Look around you. There are hundreds of different practicing religions in the world—Islam, Buddhism, Hinduism, Pantheism, Janism, Taoism, Confucianism, Judaism, and Christianity among many others. They are separate religions because there are issues about which they do not agree. Yet they are also similar in many regards.

However, to say that they are different or similar is not enough; what would be helpful is knowing *how* they are alike or different.

For example, psychology and sociology are different perspectives or approaches to studying human behavior. That is a similarity. They both use observation as a method of learning about their subjects, and they both attempt to explain people and their actions—also similarities. However, they are different in that psychology attempts to find traits, behaviors, emotions, and responses that are common to all human *individuals*, whereas sociology focuses on finding generalizations about how humans relate to one another and to society. They are both similar and different.

So, as you encounter differing beliefs or perspectives, keep in mind that they are not just similar or dissimilar; all perspectives are alike and different in important ways. Finding out how different or how similar perspectives are from one another is the task of the active learner.

Tip 4   Identify sources where multiple perspectives are expressed.

There are many locations where you are especially likely to encounter multiple perspectives. To get you started, we have listed a few of our favorites.

1. Talk to your classmates. Most people do not agree completely on much of anything. Just talking to someone else can often make you aware of different viewpoints.

2. Be attentive to current issues and the debates surrounding them. Current issues (abortion, health care, tax increases, education funding and standards, etc.) tend to receive a lot of media coverage and are good sources for studying multiple perspectives.

3. Read the letters-to-the-editor section of newspapers and magazines. These letters offer a natural forum for people debating significant issues. They frequently contain arguments for opposing viewpoints on a variety of issues.

4. Look for books whose very purpose is to present alternative perspectives. These are generally collections of articles that examine an issue (or multiple issues) from a variety of viewpoints. See for instance, *Race and Gender in the American Economy* by Susan Feiner, *Hot Topics* by Daniel Starer, any volume in the Greenhaven Press Opposing Viewpoints series or the collections in the Taking Sides series published by Dushkin, and the monthly issues of *Congressional Digest*.

QUICK REVIEW BOX

1. Understand that an expert has *a* perspective.
2. Be aware that facts don't speak for themselves.
3. Remember that perspectives are alike or different by degree.
4. Identify sources where multiple perspectives are expressed.

LOOKING BACK AND MOVING FORWARD

We hope that your journey through this book has been a lot like the mountain climbing we talked about in the first chapter—challenging but do-able, gradual but steadily moving forward, and very rewarding.

As you look back at the chapters you have studied, you will notice that obstacles to your learning can be conquered. While the tips for active learning are not all simple, you can find uses for each of them with frequent practice. We hope that you now see your teachers, texts, notes, friends, libraries, and other components of the college experience in somewhat of a different light after having read this book. They can all be useful to you as you work to understand a little more about yourself and our world.

Change is difficult and does not occur at once. Even when you have difficulties with particular tips, be excited that you are attacking those roadblocks to your learning excellence. The key to ongoing improvement as an active learner is to keep striving to improve both your attitudes and strategies. Remember:

Attitude + Strategies = Successful Active Learner.

As you look ahead to all that you will be learning, be proud of how far you have come. Sure, you still have a long way to go; we all do. But each of the small steps you have taken toward excellence in college is a personal victory. Don't dwell on what you cannot yet do: instead, feel good about the tips that you have mastered and about your *trying* to master other tips. You have plenty of time to master more and more as you practice active learning.

You know all too well that being an active learner is a lot harder than approaching your life as if you were just a huge sponge. But we hope that you now appreciate how much more rewarding active learning can be. The *process of striving for excellence* can be exhilarating, giving new meaning to being in college. As professors, we would be flattered if we have somehow helped you become your own best teacher.